"Organizations must now succeed in overcoming repeated waves of ever-faster disruptive change. But how? Professor Markides' profound strategic insights make *Organizing for the New Normal* a terrific read and a highly practical guide for anyone who must answer that question. Entertaining, deeply researched, with both inspiring and salutary case studies—it's as relevant for not-for-profits as any business."
**Tony Cohen, Member of the Charity Commission Board, UK; Chair of Barnardo's (2014–2018); CEO of FremantleMedia (2001–2012)**

"A must-read book for leaders that face a Volatile, Uncertain, Complex and Ambiguous (VUCA) world. We all already know it and we just faced it during the pandemic, but change is the only constant and it is here to stay. Fronting this reality is extremely important for all leaders and Markides' book shows the different steps and methods to build the agility needed to succeed in such an environment. This book will allow leaders to build organizations securing sustainable success with full buy-in from all the involved relevant stakeholders and, because it is not a 'cookbook on how to reach success,' it rather allows the reader to reflect and provides different tools, ready for use. We need it."
**Carsten Hellmann, CEO of ALK, Denmark, and former Executive Committee member of Sanofi and CEO of Merial**

"What gives entrepreneurs some advantage is that they instinctively know that the 'new normal' of management is now 'permanent revolution.' Professor Markides levels the playing field by sharing the secret. He diligently explores the rules of the new game and convincingly explains the tools every manager needs to win in this environment. This book is a must-read for any executive that wants to advance their career and keep their organization relevant in this age of accelerating innovation."
**Ali Parsa, Founder and CEO, Babylon Health**

# Organizing for the New Normal

*Prepare Your Company for the
Journey of Continuous Disruption*

Constantinos C. Markides

KoganPage

**Publisher's note**

Every possible effort has been made to ensure that the information contained in this book is accurate at the time of going to press, and the publishers and authors cannot accept responsibility for any errors or omissions, however caused. No responsibility for loss or damage occasioned to any person acting, or refraining from action, as a result of the material in this publication can be accepted by the publisher or the author.

First published in Great Britain and the United States in 2021 by Kogan Page Limited

| 2nd Floor, 45 Gee Street | 122 W 27th St, 10th Floor | 4737/23 Ansari Road |
| London | New York, NY 10001 | Daryaganj |
| EC1V 3RS | USA | New Delhi 110002 |
| United Kingdom | | India |
| www.koganpage.com | | |

© Constantinos C. Markides 2021

**ISBNs**

| Hardback | 9781398600805 |
| Paperback | 9781398600799 |
| Ebook | 9781398600812 |

**British Library Cataloguing-in-Publication Data**

A CIP record for this book is available from the British Library.

**Library of Congress Control Number**

2021930561

Typeset by Integra Software Services, Pondicherry
Print production managed by Jellyfish
Printed and bound by 4edge Limited, UK

# CONTENTS

# 01

# Surfing the Waves of Disruption

By all accounts, the transformation of Microsoft in 2014–2020 was dramatic and impressive. Under the leadership of Satya Nadella who took over as CEO in February 2014, the company transformed itself from a seller of packaged software—such as Windows and its suite of Office applications— to a cloud computing powerhouse, renting online storage and processing power to companies. By 2020, it had more cloud computing revenues than Google and its 17 percent cloud infrastructure market share was larger than the market share of IBM, Alibaba, and Google combined (though it was still second to Amazon's 32 percent share). Another big change was the move away from selling its suite of business applications—Word, Excel, and PowerPoint—to renting them to customers who would pay an annual licence fee. The company now boasts more than 200 million subscribers.

The transformation was not painless. It required radical cuts in the funding of Windows and Windows-based projects in order to finance the move into cloud computing. It also required letting go of investments that did not fit the new vision—for example, in 2015 the company wrote off $7.6 billion of its Nokia acquisition. More importantly, the transformation required a fundamental change in the Microsoft culture, away from everything being built around Windows to a world where Windows was just one client among many and where the company targeted its services at iPhone, Android, and Mac.

There is no question that Microsoft's transformation has—so far—been a success. Its stock price climbed by more than 200 percent in a six-year period from 2014 and its market capitalization surpassed $1 trillion on 25 April 2019. This is certainly impressive, but here is the challenge for Microsoft: Having just gone through the turmoil of one major transformation, it barely has time to take a breath or rest on its laurels. It needs to continue on the path of continuous radical change and may even have to embark on yet another major transformation. The reason is simple enough. New and even more radical disruptions—such as virtual reality, artificial intelligence (AI), machine learning, robotics, synthetic biology, nanomaterials, big data, new business models—are making their impact felt in industry after industry and changing everything along the way. Microsoft will not be immune to them and this implies that the organization must find ways to "respond" to these disruptions—not only defend against them but also exploit them in creative ways. Imagine how challenging this must be for a leader like Nadella, who just went through the painful process of rejuvenating his organization once. Just when he has "completed" one major transformation journey and maybe is thinking that it's time for the organization to get some much-needed rest, he needs to rally the troops again for more change and more turmoil.

To his credit, Nadella seems to be fully aware of this. In a May 2019 interview, he pointed out: "At Microsoft we have this very bad habit of not being able to push ourselves because we just feel very self-satisfied with the success we've had. We are learning how not to look at the past."[1] But even if he recognizes the need to not rest on his laurels, the question he must be asking himself is what exactly to do and how. He does not know which of the many disruptions swirling around Microsoft is going to grow or require his attention the most, he does not know in what form the disruption will hit them, and he does not know when it will arrive. But he somehow needs to prepare the organization both emotionally and organizationally to embark on a journey into the unknown. Again, the question is, how can he do this?

## What Is Unique About This Challenge

The need to periodically rejuvenate an organization is not new. As Figure 1.1 shows, every organization goes through a life cycle: Birth is followed by rapid growth and this, in turn, is followed by maturity. Decline will inevitably follow unless the leaders of the organization step in and rejuvenate it by moving it onto a new growth curve. This is exactly what Nadella did by moving Microsoft into cloud computing. The rejuvenation can sustain the firm for many years, but it will not last forever. At a certain point, maturity will set in and the need for rejuvenation will arise again. Therefore, rejuvenating declining organizations has been a leadership requirement since the beginning of time.

FIGURE 1.1  Periodic rejuvenation is necessary

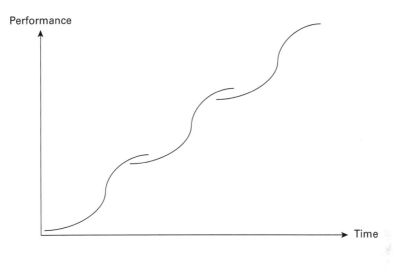

However, there is a difference now. In today's world, everything seems to be happening much more quickly. As one example of this, consider the data in Table 1.1. A century ago, it took more than 60 years for products such as airlines or cars to reach 50 million users. By contrast, at the turn of this century, it took less than five years for products such as YouTube and Facebook to achieve the same number of users. This is just one indication that change is happening at an accelerating or even exponential pace. The implication of this has been nicely summarized in *Nature* magazine: "Many things that society now takes for granted would have seemed like futuristic nonsense just a few decades ago. We can search across billions of pages, images and videos on the web; mobile phones have become ubiquitous; billions of connected smart sensors monitor in real time everything from the state of the planet to our heartbeats, sleep and steps; and drones and satellites the size of shoeboxes roam the skies. If the pace of change is exponentially speeding up, all those advances could begin to look trivial within a few years."[2]

The accelerating pace of change has an additional implication, specific to companies. It is no longer the case that companies face the growth curves depicted in Figure 1.1. Instead, they are now facing the curves shown in Figure 1.2. This basically means that whereas in the past companies could expect their rejuvenation to sustain them for years to come, this will no longer be the case. Before they have a chance to complete one rejuvenation, companies need to embark on another one. There is no time to rest, no time

TABLE 1.1  Number of years it took for products to gain 50 million users

|  | Years |
| --- | --- |
| Airlines | 68 |
| Cars | 62 |
| Phone | 50 |
| Electricity | 46 |
| Credit cards | 28 |
| Television | 22 |
| ATMs | 18 |
| Computer | 14 |
| Cell phones | 12 |
| Internet | 7 |
| YouTube | 4 |
| Facebook | 3 |
| Twitter | 2 |
| WeChat | 1 |
| Pokemon Go | 19 days |

SOURCE  Jeff Desjardins: "How long does it take to hit 50 million users?" *Visual Capitalist*, June 8, 2018.

FIGURE 1.2  Transformation in today's world

to admire their efforts, no time to think. How do you prepare the organization for continuous *and* overlapping disruptions? How do you prepare for what is coming next while you are busily driving your current transformation? And how do you convince "tired" employees to join you on the journey? This is the challenge that every leader is now facing, no matter how successful their digital transformation of the past decade has been.

My own research has alerted me to the magnitude of this challenge. In 2016–2017, I undertook a survey of 150 senior executives in big, established firms from all over the world and asked them to evaluate how successful they had been in responding to the digital disruption *of the past ten years*. The majority said they were satisfied with how they responded and assessed their efforts as "work in progress." However, when asked about their prospects, 7 out of 10 claimed to be "worried" or "very worried." There were several reasons given for this, but a key one was their perception that new disruptions were invading their businesses with increasing regularity, demanding continuous attention and resources. What worried them was the challenge of lifting their people for yet another battle so soon after the last one, and the uncertainty of developing a response to disruptions whose effects and timing were still unknown or unclear.

Instinctively, these executives knew that the nature of the task facing them now was different from simply preparing their organization to respond to a *one-off* disruption. Consider, for example, the need to create urgency for change. There is no CEO in the world who does not know that you need to create a sense of urgency in the organization before you embark on a major change journey. This is standard advice in any book on change or transformation, and is an idea that is ingrained in the DNA fabric of any graduating business school student. However, creating urgency for *continuous* transformation is not at all the same as creating urgency for a *one-off* radical change or restructuring. For a start, you have the challenge of galvanizing people who may be emotionally drained from the exertions of your ongoing digital transformation journey. More importantly, your task now is to create not just a one-off sense of urgency but a "permanent" sense of urgency—a constant unease with the status quo—that sustains the organization for the unending journey of continuous change. A burning platform will not do the trick here.

Consider also how you need to frame the need for (yet more) change to your people. Everybody seems to know that it is a mistake to frame disruption as only a threat to defend against. Disruption is both a threat and an opportunity—an idea highlighted by Clay Christensen in his book on disruptive innovation, which, according to the *Sloan Management Review*, is "one of a select handful of big management ideas the majority of executives are familiar with."[3] In fact, in a survey of 486 global CEOs that I undertook in 2019, I found that almost 96 percent of them believed that it is better to approach disruption as an opportunity rather than as a threat. The challenge, however, is to convince people who are surrounded by threatening disruptions that they should not look at them as threats but as opportunities. At a rational level, they will agree with you. But their thinking and feelings will be dominated by the fear of what disruption might do to them. It is this fear that will preoccupy them and guide their actions in the middle of the disruption. As a result, your best attempts to convince people to approach disruption as an opportunity will most likely fall on deaf ears and the majority of people will treat it as a threat. As I will explain later, this will lead to wrong actions and responses. It is therefore imperative to find ways to convince people that disruptions are indeed opportunities and should be treated as such.[4] But how do you do that? And how do you do it again and again?

## What This Book Will Cover

The purpose of this book is to explore the question: "How do you prepare the organization to respond to *continuous and overlapping* disruptions or one disruption after another in a short period of time?" Another way of saying this is: "How do you prepare the organization to be ready to engage in continuous radical change?" As I have already hinted, the challenge is complicated by the fact that you have limited time at your disposal and you are already busy with your current transformation. In addition, you are likely to be facing an organization that is emotionally tired from the transformation you are already undertaking. All this adds up to a huge and unique challenge that requires different skills and strategies from those that served us well in the past. This book will explore some of the things that leaders have to do to succeed in this. Specifically, we will explore the following issues:

- First, you need to convince your people that the disruptions coming your way are not just threats to your hard-earned success. Yes, they are threats, but they are also opportunities that need to be exploited in creative and innovative ways. Most people would claim that they have heard this advice before but unfortunately it is easier said than done. Your people are surrounded by disruptions and all they see all day are the negative consequences of these disruptions. Sure, at a rational level they can appreciate that many benefits will come their way, maybe sometime in the future. But their immediate concern is to stay alive! Their attention will be focused on the negative aspects of disruption and no matter what you say, they will "hear" or "see" only threat. How, then, can you convince people that something is positive when all they see around them is negative? We will explore this issue in Chapter 2.

- Second, you need to create a "permanent" sense of urgency that keeps your people on a constant state of alert. You don't know when the next disruption will hit so you need to be ready at all times. This means that creating a burning platform is not enough—that is how you create a one-off sense of urgency but it's definitely the wrong way to create a positive sense of constant unease with the status quo. At the same time, your people are emotionally drained and tired from the transformation you are currently undertaking. Scaring them into action will not do the trick. You have to find new ways to rally them. We will explore how to do this in Chapter 3.

- Third, you need to institutionalize the day-to-day behaviors that will allow you to not only identify quickly if a disruption is heading your way but also respond to it quickly and effectively. This sentence is a mouthful and it will take us two chapters to untangle everything that this statement implies. Suffice to say that the behaviors needed are well known to everybody, so the problem is not lack of knowledge. The problem, instead, is lack of action: Despite knowing what is expected of them, few people follow these behaviors. There are, of course, reasons for this, and we will explore what those reasons are and what can be done to get everybody in the organization to behave in ways that will make us agile and ready to embrace whatever disruption hits us, whenever. This topic will be covered in Chapter 4. We will also explore how to institutionalize these behaviors in a *decentralized* way, through the actions of managers and team leaders throughout the organization. This is a far more effective and sustainable way to change the culture of the organization than the centralized, top-down way. This topic will be covered in Chapter 5.

- Fourth, giving mid-level managers and team leaders autonomy and encouraging a decentralized change process cannot be undertaken in a vacuum. It should be obvious that granting autonomy without some constraints or guiding parameters will be a recipe for disaster. We therefore need to develop the parameters within which people can act with freedom and autonomy. The most important of these guiding parameters are the clear *strategic choices* the organization has made as to what it will do and, more importantly, what it will *not* do. This sounds simple enough, but the evidence is that organizations do not make the necessary choices that a good strategy requires, nor do they communicate their strategy clearly enough to offer guidance to their people. Another important guiding parameter is the *purpose and values* of the organization that help people decide what is right for the company and what is not. Again, this sounds easy to put in place, but the evidence is that most organizations fail to "sell" their purpose and values to their employees to win their buy-in. As a result, these remain beautiful decorations on the wall rather than becoming the guiding lighthouse for our people. We will explore how to improve this state of affairs in Chapter 6.

- Fifth, the time will come when the organization needs to develop its specific strategy to respond to whatever disruption is affecting its business. It is impossible to decide on a response strategy without knowing first what specific disruption we are responding to, but the most important thing is to ensure that our response is an innovative one. The goal should not be to defend against the disruption but to exploit it, a topic explored in Chapter 7. This raises the issue of *how* to develop an innovative response and we will consider how to achieve this in Chapter 8.

- Not only must we develop an innovative response, we must also convince our people that this is the correct response for us. In addition, no strategy will be perfect from the start, so we need to ensure that we learn from the market and adjust what we are doing accordingly. How do you know if your strategy is right and how do you convince others to support you? The answer is through experimentation, but the problem is that not all experiments are good ones, especially when it comes to experimenting with a strategy rather than a new idea or product. How can you design and carry out a "clever" experiment for your response strategy? We will answer this question in Chapter 9.

- Finally, the time will come when the organization will embark on its response strategy and the issue that will arise is how to make the transition from whatever it is doing now to what it needs to be doing in the future. Migrating to the new strategic position is a challenge and many things can go wrong along the way. We will explore how to make this transition as painlessly as possible in Chapter 10.

I hope that senior executives reading this will find nothing surprising in these steps and there should be nothing here that they do not immediately recognize. But I also hope that they are sufficiently intrigued to read further, to understand *how* to implement these steps. The contribution of my book is not the discovery of an unknown recipe for success. Instead, I will try to show that how you implement *correctly* what on paper looks obvious and common sense can be the difference between success and failure. Knowing what to do is not the same thing as doing it or doing it correctly, and this is the area where I hope my book can be useful to you.

Will reading this book make you a better leader or a better manager? This will depend not so much on whether you learn something new but on whether you translate into action any insights you develop as you read this book. The evidence is that as human beings, we very often fail to translate knowledge into action. For example, we all know we should engage in regular physical exercise, but few of us do it; we all know we should challenge and question continuously how our company operates, but we rarely do it, unless we are facing a crisis; we all know that, as leaders, we should be spending a lot of our time "thinking strategically" about our business, but the evidence is we don't. There are many reasons for this knowing–doing gap.[5] Not having enough time is one reason, and so is an organizational culture and incentives that do not encourage the desired behaviors. But another, more personal reason is the feeling of helplessness. Many times, we don't do something because we believe our actions will not make a difference. For example, can I as an individual really change the culture or the incentives of my organization? Can I really change how my people behave? If we believe that our efforts will have no or little effect, then why bother trying? One of the things that I will try to communicate in this book is the butterfly principle.[6] This states that "small changes can have a big impact." This book will highlight some of the "small things" that you can do to make a big difference in your organization. If the prospect excites you, then read on!

## References

1   Austin Carr and Dina Bass: "The most valuable company (for now) is having a Nadellaissance," *Bloomberg Business Week*, May 2, 2019.
2   Declan Butler: "Tomorrow's world," *Nature*, February 25, 2016, Vol. 530, pp. 399–401.

3  Scott D. Anthony and Paul Michelman: "The lies leaders tell themselves about disruption," Three Big Points Podcast, *Sloan Management Review*, March 3, 2020.

4  Constantinos Markides and David Lancefield: "How to convince people that a crisis is also an opportunity," *Forbes*, April 28, 2020.

5  Jeffrey Pfeffer and Robert Sutton: *The Knowing–Doing Gap: How smart companies turn knowledge into action*, Boston, MA: HBS Press, 1999.

6  This is the principle underpinning the work of Richard Thaler and Cass Sunstein: *Nudge: Improving decisions about health, wealth and happiness*, London: Penguin Books, 2009.

# 02

# Attitude Is Key

*How to Create the Right Mindset for the Journey*

There is no question that the digital revolution of the last 20 years has had a tremendous effect on how we work, how we shop, how we live our daily lives, what we value, and what we expect in life. These changes, in turn, have led companies to radically transform how they manage their employees, how they serve their customers, and how they compete with each other. For example, we have seen a shift away from hierarchy toward networks; from fixed pricing to dynamic pricing; from mass marketing to customized marketing; from close innovation to open innovation; from traditional strategies to platform strategies. The changes have been dramatic, and companies have had to transform themselves to not only survive this tsunami of digital disruption but to exploit it.

And yet, the journey is only just beginning. No matter how disruptive the digital revolution has been over the last 20 years, and no matter how much effort and how many sacrifices we have endured to respond to it, new and more disruptive changes are on the way. It is not only technological changes—such as AI, robotics, machine learning, and virtual reality—that are threatening our very survival. Geopolitical shifts—witness the rise of China—as well as macroeconomic, demographic, institutional, environmental, and health-related disruptions—think COVID-19 here—are all combining to create a cocktail of disruption that promises to make the digital disruption look like child's play by comparison.

This implies that companies need to be on constant alert, ready to respond to whatever disruption comes their way, and, if necessary, embark on yet another transformation. As a famous statement by an unknown author says:

*The end of a journey means the start of another.* This is exactly the message that needs to be communicated to the organization: Having just started or undertaken a tiring digital transformation journey, we cannot rest on our laurels, we need to embark on the next journey. This all sounds very nice and sensible, but the issue is how to convince our people to follow us. They are tired and exhausted from everything we've been doing to respond to the digital disruption, how can we stir them into action again? This is the challenge that we explore in this chapter. The key messages that I want to deliver are: (i) how we communicate to our people the need to respond to yet more disruption is important, and (ii) there is a wrong way to do it and a correct way. Failure to do it the correct way can spell trouble, no matter what strategy we adopt.

## The Importance of the Language We Use

"He told a lie, he's not a liar." That's how the actor Matthew McConaughey explained Lance Armstrong's admission that he had used illegal performance-enhancing drugs on his way to seven Tour de France victories.[1] This is an interesting statement because the communicator (McConaughey) is drawing a distinction between a behavior (he told a lie) and the identity of the person (a liar). It turns out that this is important—it makes a big difference to how people behave if we emphasize their identity rather than their behavior. Specifically, academic research has shown that you are more likely to influence people's behaviors—that is, more likely to get them to do something or change something—if you emphasize their identity rather than their actual behavior.[2] This means that instead of saying to people "do not lie," you should say "don't be a liar"; or instead of saying to them "please vote," you should tell them "be a voter."

I use this example to show how important language is in influencing human behavior. As another example of this, consider the usual advice we give to young people to "*find* their passion in life." Recent work has shown that telling people to find their passion is actually bad for them.[3] It leads them to believe that their passion is somewhere out there waiting to be discovered. As a result, they tend to become disappointed when they fail to discover it and start blaming their bad luck for the failure. Far better to tell people to *develop* their passion because that gives them the message that interests are something that anyone can cultivate through effort and time.

As a result, they become more proactive and persistent in pursuing an interest and they are more likely to grow an interest into a passion. It is truly amazing, but simply changing the statement from "find your passion" to "develop your passion" can have a huge impact on how people feel and behave.

As a final example, consider the following scenario.[4] Your doctor informs you that you are suffering from a certain form of cancer and that you have two options to fight it: radiotherapy or surgery. When you ask your doctor for her recommendation, she tells you that she cannot really recommend one or the other. But she can give you the probabilities of success for each method of treatment. One way to tell you this is the following:

> Of 100 people having surgery, 10 will die during surgery, 32 will have died by one year, and 66 will have died by five years. Of 100 people having radiation therapy, none will die during treatment, 23 will die by one year, and 78 will die by five years. Which treatment would you prefer?

In this framing, the doctor has basically told you the probabilities in terms of how many people die. She could, of course, give you the same underlying probabilities by framing the information in terms of how many people survive. Here it is:

> Of 100 people having surgery, 90 will survive the surgery, 68 will survive past one year, and 34 will survive through five years. Of 100 people having radiation therapy, all will survive the treatment, 77 will survive one year, and 22 will survive past five years. Which treatment would you prefer?

Both statements reveal the same underlying information and you'd therefore expect rational human beings to make the same choice no matter how you give them this information. Yet, in real life, the results are dramatic. When people were presented with the information in terms of dying (first scenario), there was a 50–50 split between surgery and radiotherapy. When presented with the same facts in terms of how many people survive (second scenario), 84 percent of people chose surgery.

All this brings us to disruption. It would be natural to start a book on how to respond to disruption with a description of the strategies that have been shown to lead companies to success. However, before a company embarks on any strategy, its leaders have to explain to their people "the why"—why do we have to undertake even more changes and why do we have to respond to more disruption? Have we not done enough already, and given all the changes we have undertaken in the last few years, isn't our company well positioned to weather the coming storm? Answers have to be provided and this requires communication. The evidence shows that the language used to explain to people why we should respond to disruption determines how they behave, and this can be the difference between success and failure.[5]

Most people assume that the reason we need to respond to disruption is (or should be) a no-brainer. The company is facing an existential threat so it is only natural that we should do something about it. They therefore believe that the obvious way to explain to people "the why" is to first describe the specific disruption that is undermining the business, emphasize to them the mortal danger the organization is facing, and then ask for their help and support in responding to this danger. This is a *threat* framing, analogous to a doctor telling you: "If you do not stop smoking and begin exercising on a regular basis, you will start having serious health problems and you will die prematurely." However, there is an alternative way to explain to people the need for change. Instead of scaring them into action, you give them a positive vision of what can be achieved if they do embark on the change you are proposing, and so you galvanize them to join you on this journey of discovery. This is an *opportunity* framing, analogous to the doctor telling you: "If you stop smoking and start exercising on a regular basis, you will live to be 100 without major health problems or health scares."

Given these two possible ways of framing the need for change to employees, the challenge for senior leaders is which one to pick: Should they frame it as a threat that we need to defend against or as an opportunity to attack and exploit? It seems that most of us instinctively lean toward the positive framing—in a survey of 486 global CEOs that we conducted in 2019, almost 96 percent said that companies that frame disruption as an opportunity rather than as a threat are more likely to succeed with their responses to disruption. This belief is actually wrong.

The doctoral dissertation work of Clark Gilbert at Harvard Business School examined the response of the US newspaper industry to the arrival of the internet and online distribution of news. Not surprisingly, he found that those companies that viewed the internet as a threat ended up failing in their response. Perhaps more surprisingly, he did not find that those companies that viewed it as an opportunity succeeded with their response—in fact, they also failed. His surprising finding was that the companies that ended up developing successful response strategies were those that framed disruption as both a threat and an opportunity.[6]

This may strike readers as academic nit-picking, but there is a good rationale behind such a finding. Viewing something as a threat has both benefits and costs—on the plus side, it helps us develop a sense of urgency in the organization and focuses our mind and resources on the task at hand. On the minus side, it makes us rely more on instinct rather than analysis and we prioritize the short term over the long term. For example, consider what happens when a lion attacks you while you are out on safari. The clear and present danger of the advancing lion creates urgency, focuses the mind, and galvanizes resources to respond to the lion. This is all positive, but something negative also happens—we react to the danger without really thinking and we focus on short-term solutions. All this to suggest that seeing something as a threat has both positives and negatives. Needless to say, viewing something as an opportunity also has benefits and costs—on the plus side, it helps us think about the issues logically, analytically, and with a long-term perspective, but on the minus side, it fails to create the necessary sense of urgency that leads to action. This implies that if we want to achieve both urgency and long-term thinking in the organization, we need to frame disruption as both a threat and an opportunity.

## An Example: New Disruptive Business Models

This point becomes obvious when we look at one specific disruption that is affecting numerous companies: the arrival of a new and disruptive business model in an established market. If there is one thing we know about disruptive business models it is that they grow by attracting two different types of customers: the customers that are currently served by the established companies, and entirely new customers that enter the market for the first time. In fact, as demonstrated by Clay Christensen in his work on disruptive innovation, it is *new* customers that originally are attracted to the invading business model and give it the initial support that it needs to grow.[7] It is only over time that established customers find the new thing "good enough" and switch to it. The process through which new business models grow is shown in Figure 2.1, which is adapted from the work of Clark Gilbert.[8]

FIGURE 2.1   How new disruptive business models grow

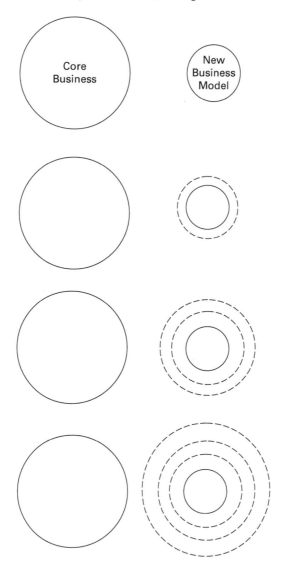

FIGURE 2.1  (Continued)

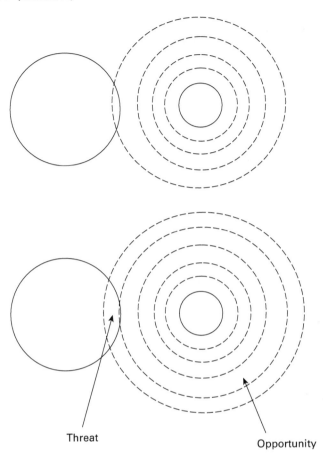

Threat

Opportunity

SOURCE Adapted from Clark Gilbert: "The disruption opportunity," *Sloan Management Review*, Summer 2003, Vol. 44, No. 4, p. 28.

When it arrives, the new business model attracts customers that are different from the customers of the core business. For example, the first customers that were attracted to the online brokerage business model were day traders rather than wealthy or institutional investors. Similarly, the first customers attracted to the low-cost, point-to-point airline business model were bargain-hunting families and students rather than the business traveler. These "different" customers are what sustain the new business model in the short term, but the innovators who introduced the business model keep improving it year after year until it reaches a point that it becomes "good enough" for the customers of the core business. That's when these core customers begin to switch to the new model and that is when the cannibalization of the core business begins. This process goes on for some time and the end result is shown in Figure 2.2. Here we see that the market created by disruption (the shaded circle) is composed of two types of customers—customers of the established core business and new customers (different from the customers of the established business).

Figure 2.2 should make it immediately obvious that the new business model is both a threat and an opportunity for the established firms. It is a threat because it attracts some of the customers from the core business and in the process cannibalizes the core; and it is an opportunity because it creates a new market composed of entirely new customers.

FIGURE 2.2   A new disruptive business model is both a threat and an opportunity

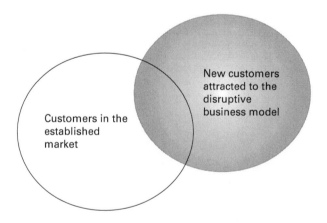

## Why It's Important to See Disruption as
## Both a Threat and an Opportunity

One might wonder what the fuss is all about. What difference does it make how we look at disruption? Is this much ado about nothing? Part of the answer, as already suggested, is that we will achieve urgency *and* long-term thinking only when we look at disruption as both a threat and an opportunity rather than as an either/or. However, there are other benefits that flow from the correct framing of the issue. What we know is that how we frame something will determine how we think about it, how we approach it, and what we do in the end. This might determine whether we succeed or fail in our response.

For example, if disruption is both a threat and an opportunity, the first implication for companies is that they need to both defend and attack disruption. This immediately raises the question: Can a company defend and attack with one strategy? Perhaps it is better to have two different strategies—one that aims to protect the core and a second one that aims to exploit the new markets created by disruption? This is the topic of dual transformation that has already been explored by academics[9] and which we will explore later in the book, in Chapter 8. Furthermore, if two different strategies are needed, can the managers of the core business develop both of them, or should the development of the "attack" strategy be assigned to different people? Finally, if two different strategies are needed to "respond" to disruption, should they both be implemented by the same company or should a separate unit be given the task of executing the attack strategy? These are obviously difficult questions and we do not pretend to have all the answers. But the point is that the "correct" questions can be asked only if we start our thinking with the "right" attitude toward disruption.

As a further example of the importance of approaching disruption with the "correct" attitude, consider one of the most accepted principles of good management—that companies should listen to their customers. In my CEO survey administered in 2019, almost 88 percent of CEOs found the following statement to be true: *Companies that are close to their core customers and listen to them tend to do better in responding to disruption.* Yet, looking at disruption as both a threat and an opportunity should alert you to the shortcomings in this position.

On the face of it, this statement sounds obviously true—after all, how can a company succeed without paying attention to its core customers? Yet, when it comes to disruption, this may prove counterproductive. This is because, as we said above, many of the customers that are attracted to the disruption are not our core or existing customers; they are *new* customers, many of them attracted into the market for the first time. It is therefore not enough to listen to our existing customers—in fact, Christensen's work on disruptive innovation has shown that listening to the existing customers may lead a company astray.[10]

Consider, for example, the mid-1990s when online brokerage emerged as a viable business model, with companies such as Charles Schwab and E-Trade leading the charge. Imagine that in response to the early success of this way of competing, a traditional broker like Merrill Lynch approached its existing customers—the wealthy individuals or institutional investors— and offered them online brokerage. Basically, just like any other online broker, it would offer them cheaper prices and quicker execution but with no or limited service or research and advice. It is highly unlikely that wealthy individuals or institutional investors would want to switch from Merrill Lynch's traditional offering of service and advice (for a fee) to an offering of no advice in return for lower fees. They would say as much to Merrill Lynch and as a result the company would feel no need to adopt the new business model. In this sense, listening to the existing customers might lead you away from something that might grow to become a profitable business. Even if the existing customers don't lead us astray, paying attention only to this group of customers will yield ideas that are primarily aimed at defending the core business. It is only talking to the new customers and understanding the different things they expect and want that will allow us to develop ideas for how to attack and exploit the disruption.

Similarly, it is only when we approach disruption as both a threat and an opportunity that we appreciate the need to go beyond improving our current offerings and service. As outlined above, the academic research on disruptive innovation has shown that the markets created by disruption are originally comprised of different customers from the ones that buy from the established firms.[11] These customers do not want what the established firms are offering—they want the "new" things that disruptors emphasize. This suggests that by trying to improve what it is already offering, the established firm is unlikely to attract these different customers—they want different things, not the same things, even if they are better.

Nor can the established firm expect to win against disruptors by offering the same but better products as those the disruptors are already offering. The disruptors are the "first movers" in the new markets that disruption has created—simply attacking by trying to be better than them will most likely end in failure. As Michael Porter proposed: "The cardinal rule in offensive strategy is not to attack head-on with an imitative strategy, regardless of the challenger's resources or staying power."[12] All this suggests that trying to be "better" is not a good response to disruption. The established firm ought to start its thinking like an entrepreneur who is about to enter a market totally new to them and design a strategy that's appropriate for the new market. This new strategy is unlikely to be a better version of what the established firm is already using in its core markets.

These are all examples to show that how we frame disruption to our people will act as the "lens" through which they will look at the challenges they are facing. This, in turn, will determine what questions they will ask and what answers they will pursue. Framing disruption the "correct" way—as both a threat and an opportunity—will increase the probability that our people will ask the "correct" questions.

## How to Convince Employees That Disruption Is an Opportunity

This brings us to what is perhaps the biggest challenge that leaders face in framing disruption as both a threat and an opportunity to their people. Most of us will intuitively accept the argument that we should frame it both ways, and in fact, the majority of CEOs we interviewed about their digital transformation journeys in 2018–2019 claimed to have communicated as much to their organization. The following quote captures this sentiment well: "Artificial Intelligence will create millions more jobs than it will destroy."[13]

While all this makes perfect sense, the problem we face is that people are receiving this message in a context of destruction brought about by the disruption, including job losses. We may be encouraging them to see disruption as an opportunity but all they see around them every day are the negative consequences of disruption. For example, as I am writing these words, the world is engulfed in the COVID-19 crisis. Many people are talking of the need to not just focus on the negative effects of this crisis but to also appreciate the positives—for example, how many of us will learn to work remotely or in a virtual way. This, of course, makes rational sense, but it's of little comfort to all of us whose primary concern is to survive this crisis.

Consider another example. Imagine that you were just fired by your company. Imagine, further, that when you got home, your loved ones tried to convince you that even though this was a bad outcome (and maybe a threat to your financial well-being), it was also a great opportunity for you—perhaps to learn a new skill, or to spend more time with the family, or to embark on that travel around the world you've always wanted to undertake but never found the time for. There is no question that at a rational level, you can see the many benefits associated with your newfound free time, and you may even feel better about your predicament. But how long will this pleasant feeling last or how long will it take for you to start worrying about your future again? More importantly, what would you spend most of your time doing in the next few months—trying to find another job or traveling around the world?

The fact that, compared with the future benefits that disruption might bring, people put more weight on its immediate negative consequences, which they see and feel now, has a serious implication for how we communicate and describe disruption to our employees. Specifically, more time and more effort need to be spent explaining to people why disruption is an opportunity rather than a threat. A 50–50 time split, or using similar communication strategies, is not enough. In practice, this means that to make the case that disruption is a threat, you will have to provide a clear articulation of the specific challenges facing the organization, along with the choices and trade-offs, supported by the facts. However, to make the case that disruption is also an opportunity requires much more than communication or pointing out the facts. People need to buy into the idea that disruption is an opportunity at an emotional level if they are to give it the attention it deserves.

All this suggests that convincing people that something is "positive" when they are in the midst of something "negative" is extremely difficult. The challenge, therefore, is not to tell or communicate to people that disruption is an opportunity—it is, instead, to *convince* them that this is the case when all they see are threatening developments around them. How, then, can you "sell" the idea that disruption is an opportunity to an audience that is predisposed to seeing or valuing primarily the negative? We will offer a way to think about it in the next chapter. The most important thing to appreciate is that selling something requires much more than communication. For people to "buy into" something—both at a rational and an emotional level—many tactics over and above effective communication should be employed. Unless you are as inspirational as Martin Luther King, chances are that communication will not be enough to win your employees' hearts—hence the need for additional tactics, such as visualization, stories, rituals, symbolic actions, early victories, and the development of a supportive organizational environment.

## An Example: KBC Bank

An example here may help illuminate the issues. Belgium's KBC Bank is considered one of Europe's best banks. Since 2015, it has been collecting annual "best of" awards, including Euromoney's "World's Best Bank in Western Europe" in 2019. It wasn't always like this. In fact, the bank needed a bailout by the Belgian government during the 2008–2009 financial crisis and another one from both the federal government in Belgium and the Flemish government in its region during the euro crisis of 2011–2012. At the time that Johan Thijs became the CEO in 2012, the bank was close to bankruptcy. Thijs undertook a series of transformations, first in 2012 and then again in 2016, to bring the bank back from the dead and make it Europe's best. Asked how he motivates his people to engage in these transformations, his reply is as follows:

> First, I never talk to them about the bank or what the bank needs to do. Instead, I talk about them as human beings, as consumers. For example, I would ask my people: Have you bought a smartphone recently? If so, tell me what you do with it. Do you use it to shop or to search for information or to pay for parking? Do you take it with you all the time and use it all the time? Do you use Siri to help you in your daily life? Once they appreciate how technology is affecting how we live our life, how we work and how we shop, I then ask them whether the same thing will happen in how people do their banking. I implore them to ask themselves: If this is happening in everything we do, why not in banking? If *you* behave differently now, why not our consumers? This is scary! People immediately realize that our industry will not be spared. They realize that companies like Google and Amazon will kill us. But at that point, I would jump in and offer them a possible solution. How about if we do this or that? For example, how about if our bank develops a voice-activated digital assistant for our consumers that is embedded in our bank's mobile app? The consumers carry their smartphones with them all the time, so, in effect, they are carrying our digital assistant with them. Every time they need to undertake a transaction, they can do it with our app. If they want to pay for their parking or buy train tickets or pay for an expensive TV, all they have to do is talk to our app. Everything is taken care of in seconds. This gets my people excited! They realize that it's not all doom and gloom, that we can fight back and carve out a future

for ourselves. What gets them excited is the realization that we are not offering them just empty words and fanciful promises. We are offering them tangible products or tangible actions that we can take to respond. Do they want to work with us to develop and implement these solutions? You bet! They cannot wait to get started!

Thijs makes it sound easy, but selling an idea so that people buy into it is diffi-cult and time consuming. It is a process that requires constant attention and continuous reinforcement. It requires effective communication but also actions that reinforce and legitimize what we are selling to people. It needs the contin-uous and visible support of people at the top. Now, compare what is needed to convince people that a disruption is an opportunity with what is needed to make the case that disruption is a threat. It should come as no surprise to know that most organizations do not allocate the requisite time and attention to do this and instead opt to simply communicate to their people that disruption is not just a threat but also an opportunity. Unsurprisingly, people only "hear" the threat framing and organizations end up focusing on defending rather than exploiting the disruption.

This comes at a huge cost to the organization. As demonstrated by Clark Gilbert, organizations that frame disruption as a threat end up failing in their responses.[14] A little more investment up front in how the disruption is positioned and communicated to the organization could save the company a lot of money and heartache later on.

# References

1   Julie Miller: "Matthew McConaughey has come to terms with Lance Armstrong's doping confession," *Vanity Fair*, March 22, 2013.

2   Christopher Bryan, Gabrielle Adams, and Benoit Monin: "When cheating would make you a cheater: Implicating the self prevents unethical behaviour," *Journal of Experimental Psychology: General*, 2013, Vol. 142, No. 4, pp. 1001–1005.

3   Paul O'Keefe, Carol Dweck, and Gregory Walton: "Implicit theories of interest: Finding your passion or developing it?" *Psychological Science*, 2018, Vol. 29, No. 10, pp. 1653–1664.

4   As described in Barbara J. McNeil, Stephen G. Pauker, Harold Sox, and Amos Trevsky: "On the elicitation of preferences for alternative therapies," *New England Journal of Medicine*, May 27, 1982, Vol. 306, No. 21, pp. 1259–1262.

5    Clark Gilbert and Joseph Bower: "Disruption: The art of framing," *Harvard Business School Working Knowledge*, June 10, 2002; Clark Gilbert: "The disruption opportunity," *Sloan Management Review*, Summer 2003, Vol. 44, No. 4.

6    Clark Gilbert and Joseph Bower: "Disruption: The art of framing," *Harvard Business School Working Knowledge*, June 10, 2002; Clark Gilbert: "The disruption opportunity," *Sloan Management Review*, Summer 2003, Vol. 44, No. 4.

7    Clayton Christensen: *The Innovator's Dilemma: When new technologies cause great firms to fail*, Boston, MA: Harvard Business School Press, 1997.

8    Clark Gilbert: "The disruption opportunity," *Sloan Management Review*, Summer 2003, Vol. 44, No. 4.

9    Scott Anthony, Clark Gilbert, and Mark Johnson: *Dual Transformation: How to reposition today's business while creating the future*, Boston, MA: Harvard Business Review Press, 2017.

10   Clayton Christensen: *The Innovator's Dilemma: When new technologies cause great firms to fail*, Boston, MA: Harvard Business School Press, 1997.

11   Clayton Christensen: *The Innovator's Dilemma: When new technologies cause great firms to fail*, Boston, MA: Harvard Business School Press, 1997; Clark Gilbert and Joe Bower: "Disruptive change: When trying harder is part of the problem," *Harvard Business Review*, May 2002, pp. 3–8.

12   Michael Porter: *Competitive Advantage*, New York: Free Press, 1985, p. 514.

13   Byron Reese: "AI will create millions more jobs than it will destroy," *Singularity Hub*, January 1, 2019.

14   Clark Gilbert and Joe Bower: "Disruptive change: When trying harder is part of the problem," *Harvard Business Review*, May 2002, pp. 3–8.

# 03

# Create Urgency
# for Continuous Change

*Doing It the Right Way*

In his book *Change or Die*, Alan Deutschman reports a truly amazing statistic: After undergoing coronary artery bypass grafting, most people—not surprisingly—attempt to improve their health by undertaking radical changes to their lifestyle, for example eating a healthier diet or quitting smoking or exercising more. However, people slowly start to drift back to old habits and—here is the amazing thing—90 percent end up with the same lifestyle as before within two years of their operation.[1] Take a moment to absorb this information. There are two insights that immediately pop out. First, change is hard. It is so hard that even fear of death is not enough to convince people to change for good. Second, scare tactics can be used to create urgency for change, but such tactics will only create change that is short-lived. Unless we continuously engage in "scaring" people, they will slowly overcome their initial fear and revert to old habits. These insights have immediate applicability in business: Yes, we need a sense of urgency to encourage change in our organization, but *how* we create urgency matters.[2] There is a right way to create urgency for change and a wrong way. Choosing the "right" way is essential if we are to succeed with our transformation program.

What is the "right" way? The example above highlights a way of creating urgency which is definitely not the right way. Specifically, scaring people into change is not the right way. As we saw in this example, scare tactics produced a short-term reaction from people, but that was not sustainable. At least in this case, the change generated—albeit short-term—was in the right direction, in that people stopped smoking and started exercising. But this cannot

FIGURE 3.1  When do companies undertake radical change?

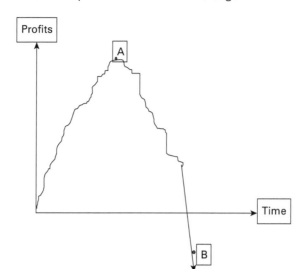

be taken for granted. Consider, for example, the popular analogy of the burning platform. There is no question that the burning platform creates urgency that leads to action, but what is the nature of that action? It is people jumping into the sea in a panicky and uncoordinated way—surely this is not the kind of urgency that we want in our organization? Similarly, consider a company facing the scenario in Figure 3.1 and ask yourselves *when* this company would consider undertaking radical action. The answer is closer to point B than to point A because that is when there is urgency for action. But again, what kinds of actions will the urgency at point B create? Most likely myopic, reactive, short-term, and non-thinking actions—exactly how you, too, would react if a lion suddenly attacked you.

I am highlighting fear and scare tactics as a particularly bad way to create urgency because this has become the standard strategy that companies adopt to generate urgency. For example, in our CEO survey, 74 percent of CEOs found the following statement to be true: "To create a sense of urgency, you have to make your people appreciate the imminent threat of disruption and the mortal danger the company is facing." This suggests that many of us believe that using scare tactics can be an effective way to create urgency—hence the popularity of the "burning platform" analogy. Yet, as we argue above, nothing can be further from the truth.

## What Is the Right Way to Create Urgency?

We therefore return to our original question: What is the "right" way to create urgency for change? To get a glimpse of the answer, consider the following story. Several years ago, in New York, I met a senior executive who worked at a major bank. He told me that for years his doctors tried to convince him to change his lifestyle because he was suffering from a rare heart disease. Nothing seemed to get to him until the day his wife sat him down and described to him in vivid language the wedding day of their two-year-old daughter, sometime in the future. She described how proud he looked, walking his daughter down the aisle, and how happy he was, dancing the night away. He said that the story had a big impact on him—in his own words: "It was as if a light switch had been turned on!" Something inside him told him that he needed to change and he embarked upon a journey of personal change immediately. Fifteen years later, he was still going strong. This is a simple story that highlights something that psychologists have been telling us for years: To create the "right" kind of urgency and get people to change for good, you need to make the need for change positive, personal, and emotional.[3] There are three requirements here and it is important to appreciate what each implies.

The first requirement is to make the need for change *positive*. This does not mean that we can ignore the bad stuff and focus only on the positive. As suggested in the previous chapter, you need to tell people the bad stuff—that is, the dire consequences of *not* responding to the disruption. However, we cannot stop there. We need to also tell them the positive stuff—that is, the wonderful things that will happen if we do respond to the disruption. This is not an either/or choice. Just like it is not enough to use only scare tactics, it is also not enough to just make the need for change positive—we need to do both.

The second requirement is to make the need for change *personal* and that means aligning the change with something that is of value to each and every single employee. This implies that it is not enough to argue for change because it will make the company more profitable or less likely to fail; people need to understand what's in it for them. After all, they are the ones bearing the costs of change, they want to see some personal benefits out of it. These benefits do not need to be monetary—in fact, non-monetary benefits are more likely to motivate people into sustainable change.

The third and most difficult requirement is to make the need for change *emotional*. This is not the same thing as making the need for change personal. Yes, employees are more likely to connect at an emotional level with a personal rather than an impersonal reason for change, but this is not guaranteed. Work still needs to be done to make even a personal reason for change emotional. It is easy to come up with a nice-sounding, positive reason why we need to change—for example, "we are doing this for our customers," or "we are doing it for society." These reasons may sound good, but the trick is to "sell" them to people to win their emotional commitment. This brings us back to the challenge we identified in the previous chapter—how do you convince people amidst all the destruction associated with disruption that positive things will eventually come our way, and more importantly, how do you get them to accept these positive things not only at a rational but also at an emotional level? In the previous chapter, I suggested that more time and effort should be spent on portraying disruption as an opportunity rather than as a threat. This would go a long way to convincing people that responding to disruption can bring positive effects. However, we still need to get our people to accept these positive outcomes at an *emotional* level.

Selling to win emotional commitment is a generic leadership challenge. In this chapter, we are talking about selling "a positive reason for change" to win our people's emotional commitment to change, but leaders need to do this kind of selling for a number of things—for example, they need to sell their strategy, or vision, or the organization's purpose, or its values. These things—strategy, vision, purpose—are meaningless unless people buy into them, and for people to buy into anything, somebody has to "sell" it to them.

Needless to say, winning people's emotional commitment is extremely difficult. For example, assume for a minute that you bought into the argument that you need to make the need for change personal and emotional, and that in response to your employees asking you "why do we need to change?" you give them a reason that is personal to them. Specifically, you tell them: "By changing, you will be helping make the world a better place for our children." This is nice, positive, and personal—exactly what you want. But how do you make it *emotional* to people? If there is one thing we know, it is that simply communicating it to people will almost never achieve the emotional response we want. After all, how many of us won the "hearts" of our partners using only communication or fancy PowerPoint presentations? Winning people's hearts for change is not easy. This may explain why so many change programs fail. It is easy to come up with a nice-sounding, positive reason why we need to change. However, how many organizations spend the time and resources to "sell" this reason to their employees to win not only their rational acceptance but also their emotional commitment to it? Doing so requires us to use not only inspiring speeches and presentations but also other tactics and strategies. It is hard, but this is the only way to create the right kind of urgency in an organization.

## How to Win Emotional Commitment

We come now to the heart of the matter: We know that to create the right kind of urgency, we need to give people a positive and personal reason why they need to change and then sell this reason to them to win their emotional commitment to it. But how do you do that? Specifically, how do you sell a positive (and personal) reason to people to win their *emotional* commitment to it? To appreciate what needs to happen, imagine calling all your people together and telling them that given all the disruptions happening around us, "we need to change." The key question in people's mind will be: "Why do we need to change? What will we achieve by changing?" Your answer to the "why" question must meet two key requirements.

### Make the Need for Change Personal

First, give them all the negative facts about disruption and warn them that if we don't change, bad things will happen to us. This is the threat framing that is necessary to demonstrate that we are not hiding from reality. But as already pointed out, you should not stop there. Complement this threat framing with a positive reason why we need to change. The key is to make sure this positive reason is *personal* to every single employee.

This, obviously, is a challenge. Different people are motivated by different things, so how can you come up with a (positive) reason that everybody would find personally meaningful? The answer is to find a "common denominator." In other words, find something that most people would relate to or most people would find worthwhile. To get an idea of what this could be, consider the following examples:

- A high-tech company explained to its employees the need for a major investment in a new product in this manner: We need to do this because 50 years from now, you will be telling your grandchildren: "I was there."

- A mining company explained to its people the need for radical changes in its safety procedures like this: We need to do this because we want you to finish work every day and go back to your family every night, safe and sound.

- A pharmaceutical company explained to its employees why they had to become more innovative in these words: You will be helping us keep more people healthy so they can spend more time with their families.

- A US-based skincare company explained to its employees why it had to undertake painful cost cuts in this manner: You will be helping our customers—the teenagers of America—live a normal life.

- A chemicals company explained to its people the need for radical change in its environmental and safety procedures like this: We need to do this so that our children and grandchildren can enjoy our lakes and rivers.

These examples point to certain things that could serve as "common denominators"—things like customers, co-workers, family, society, environment. They may not strike people as "personal," but they are certainly more personal than the usual reasons companies give for change—to help the company survive the disruption or remain profitable.

## Make the Need for Change Emotional

Giving people something personal to aim for is useful but it is hardly emotional. Even the best-sounding personal reasons will fail to elicit an emotional reaction unless you support the statement with some other tactics. If you don't believe me, consider the following statement: "Our purpose is to make the world a better place for our children and grandchildren." This is an actual purpose statement by a European multinational. There is no question that it is nice and positive, but how many of us would immediately believe that this is an honest statement, let alone be prepared to fight for its achievement with passion and energy? The answer is not many. A statement, however nice or inspiring, will not *by itself* elicit emotion from people. We therefore need to go beyond simply communicating to people to doing certain other things to support what we say. Here are a few tactics illustrating what we could be doing:

- *Walk the talk*: It should be obvious that we need to support what we are saying with actions. Nothing could be more persuasive to people than seeing their senior leaders behave in ways that support what they are proclaiming, especially when the actions are not cost-free. It will take a lot of actions and a lot of time to do this, which implies that you should not expect buy-in from people from the word go.

- *Visualization*: Things that people see are more likely to evoke emotions than things they hear or read. You should therefore help them visualize what you are trying to sell to them. This suggests that instead of simply telling them, "We need to become customer-centric because that will make our customers happy," it is better to show them a video of happy customers complimenting the company on its customer responsiveness. Similarly, instead of telling them, "We need to become more innovative because that would save people's lives," it is better to bring patients into the organization to tell the employees how your company's products have saved their lives.

A good example of the power of visualization is provided by David Pottruck, the former CEO of Charles Schwab. In 1995, Schwab had two divisions offering online trading to customers at different price points. Pottruck wanted to change that to a single price for the online offering but was not sure how to convince the organization. In his own words:[4]

> We had done the projections and knew that without the pricing change, our lead in the marketplace would soon evaporate. But numbers don't necessarily persuade or excite people… To convince the team that Schwab's position wasn't as secure as some might think, I reached out to four of the disgruntled customers who had written me letters detailing their frustrations with the tiered pricing system then in place. I asked them to meet with our leadership team to tell them about their grievances. With each of these high-revenue customers right in front of them, describing in detail how they felt the company was doing them a disservice and eroding their trust in the process, the problem became hard to ignore… These stories, delivered in person and with great passion, were far more persuasive than any tidy columns of numbers on a spreadsheet might have been."

- *Story-telling*: Stories and how you tell them are more likely to evoke emotions than a presentation. You should therefore support what you are selling to people with stories. For example, imagine visiting your doctor who determines that you are suffering from a terrible disease. Thankfully, she informs you that there are two possible medications to fight your disease: medication A that is 90 percent effective and medication B that is 30 percent effective. Assuming the two medications cost the same and have the same side effects, which one would you choose? The answer is obviously medication A. Now imagine a different scenario. You go to your doctor who informs you of your disease and then tells you only about medication A. In addition, she supplements the factual information (that medication A is 90 percent effective) with a negative story. She tells you that as your doctor, she has to make it clear to you that even though medication A is very effective, it is not perfect. In fact, this medication was given to another patient only last week and his condition did not improve. Will this additional information—the story of another patient who took medication A and did not improve—change the likelihood of you accepting medication A? In other words, will a single negative story reduce your willingness to take this medication?

Most of us would like to believe that we will not be affected by a single story, that we will base our decision on just the facts. Yet, in a simulation study where this scenario was presented to people, the number of people saying they would still take medication A declined by almost 56 percent. This is quite an amazing decline given the fact that only one story was used. The results of the complete study are presented in Figure 3.2. There are four scenarios in this simulation.[5] The first scenario is when the patients are given the facts about medication A together with a positive story—in which case, 88 percent choose to take medication A. In the second scenario, the patients are given the facts about medication A but this time the facts are complemented with a negative story. This is the scenario I described above. The number of people willing to take medication A drops to 39 percent. In the third scenario, patients are presented the facts about medication B together with a negative story—in which case, only 7 percent choose to take medication B. In the fourth and final scenario, the patients are presented the facts about medication B but this time the facts are complemented with a positive story. The number of people willing to take medication B jumps to 78 percent, a quite amazing increase simply because a positive story was told.

An equally impressive result emerges in a simulation undertaken in the context of a jury trial where the jury has to decide whether a subject is guilty of first-degree murder.[6] The results are shown in Figure 3.3. When both the prosecution and the defense teams present just facts, the subject gets indicted 63 percent of the time. When they both present stories, the subject gets indicted 59 percent of the time. But see what happens when the prosecution uses facts and the defense uses stories—indictment drops to 31 percent. By contrast, indictment jumps to 78 percent when defense uses facts while

FIGURE 3.2  The power of stories—a medical example

|  | Negative story | Positive story |
| --- | --- | --- |
| Medication A 90% effective | 39% | 88% |
| Medication B 30% effective | 7% | 78% |

Base rate information

SOURCE  Angela Freymuth and George Ronan: "Modeling patient decision-making: The role of base-rate and anecdotal information," *Journal of Clinical Psychology in Medical Settings*, September 2004, Vol. 11, No. 3.

the prosecution uses stories. These are all results that highlight how important story-telling is in influencing people's judgment and decisions.

It should be obvious that to win people's emotional commitment, many tactics over and above effective communication should be employed. It should also be obvious that this is a time-consuming process that requires a lot of effort and energy on the part of senior management. If we were to compare what is needed to try to create urgency through scare tactics versus what is needed to try to create it by making an emotional case for it, one

FIGURE 3.3  The power of stories—a legal example

| | Prosecution Facts | Prosecution Story |
| --- | --- | --- |
| Defense Facts | 63% | 78% |
| Defense Story | 31% | 59% |

SOURCE  Nancy Pennington and Reid Hastie: "Explanation-based decision-making: Effects of memory structure on judgment," *Journal of Experimental Psychology: Learning, Memory and Cognition*, 1988, Vol. 14, pp. 521–533.

could see why organizations prefer the easier and quicker strategy of scare tactics. The strategy of fear may be easier to utilize, but it is almost never as effective as the strategy of making the need for change emotional to people.

## What Determines Selling Effectiveness

If you succeed in winning your people's emotional commitment to the reason you have given them for change, you will have succeeded in creating a positive sense of urgency in the organization. We have identified several tactics that you can use in selling, but *how* you sell something is only one of the factors that determine selling effectiveness. A vast literature on the diffusion of innovations has alerted us to several other factors that can influence whether we would be successful in selling our ideas successfully.[7] Specifically, we know that selling effectiveness is determined by five key factors (see Figure 3.4). These are:

- The *seller* of the innovation or idea. Some people are better at selling than others. This means that everything else equal, the good sellers will have a higher probability of success. There are several things that characterize effective sellers, such as their credibility, their authenticity, and how homophilous they are perceived to be to the buyers—that is, whether the buyers see them as "one of us."

- The *context* in which the selling takes place. For example, have you timed the introduction of the idea at a favorable time? Does the idea fit with the prevailing norms, values, and beliefs of the organization? Is there an "urgent" need for the idea? In addition, do not forget that you recently underwent another change process. Have you accounted for any unfulfilled promise in that effort and have you put the current effort in the proper context, relative to the success of the previous effort?

- The innovation or *idea* itself. Some ideas are easier to push through than others. Other things equal, the ideas that spread quickly tend to be compatible with what we are already doing, not very complex, easy to test, and seen as "good" ideas with many benefits relative to their cost. In addition, if the employees were involved in the development of the ideas and initiatives, and if they feel that they were "heard" and were considered as part of the problem-solving process, they will be more likely to accept the ideas and commit to their successful implementation.

FIGURE 3.4  What determines which ideas "spread"

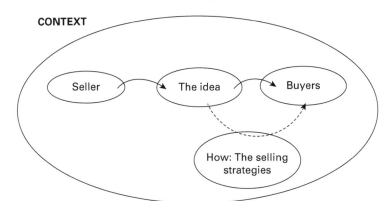

- *How* the seller is trying to "sell" the innovation. For example, have you created a positive sense of urgency? Have you framed the need for change correctly? Have you enlisted allies to help you? Are you generating early victories to create momentum?

- Who the *buyers* of the innovation are. You need to consider who the buyers are and why they should buy the idea being proposed. You also have to consider different strategies for different buyers.

Any one of these five factors (or a combination) may determine whether you will be successful in selling the need for change to the organization. It is true that people tend to focus on the "how" and put all of their energies into making sure they have the right strategies to sell their ideas. This is a mistake. All five of these factors are important and focusing on only one of them can be a recipe for disaster. All five are important and you should think strategically about them all, so as to influence them to your advantage and so increase the probability that your selling will be effective.

## References

1  Alan Deutschman: *Change or Die: Could you change when change matters most?*, New York: Regan Books, 2007.
2  John Kotter: *Leading Change*, Boston, MA: HBS Press, 1996.
3  Chip Heath: "Making the emotional case for change: An interview with Chip Heath," *McKinsey Quarterly*, 2010, No. 2.

4  David S. Pottruck: *Driving Disruption: An operator's manual*, San Francisco, CA: Maroch Hale Publishing House, 2019, pp. 59–60.

5  Angela Freymuth and George Ronan: "Modeling patient decision-making: The role of base-rate and anecdotal information," *Journal of Clinical Psychology in Medical Settings*, September 2004, Vol. 11, No. 3.

6  Nancy Pennington and Reid Hastie: "Explanation-based decision-making: Effects of memory structure on judgment," *Journal of Experimental Psychology: Learning, Memory and Cognition*, 1988, Vol. 14, pp. 521–533.

7  Everett M. Rogers: *Diffusion of Innovations, Fifth Edition*, New York: Free Press, 2003.

# 04

# Prepare for Any Disruption

*How to Develop the Behaviors of Agility*

More than 200 years ago, a class of 10-year-old German students were asked by their teacher to solve a seemingly difficult problem: "Add all the numbers from 1 to 100 and tell me the sum total." Most of us will probably do a quick search on Google to find the answer to such a problem. But assume for a minute that you don't have Google and you don't know the formula that will help you calculate the sum. How would you approach the problem? If you are at all typical of the thousands of MBA students and executives that I've given this problem to over the past 30 years, you will probably start adding the numbers linearly (that is 1+2+3+4 and so on) and then give up in frustration after a few minutes. You will then sit idly, waiting for someone to give you the answer, all the while making yourself feel good about the whole experience by saying to yourself: "Who cares?"

It turns out that one of those 10-year-old kids in the German classroom came up with the answer really quickly. Instead of adding the numbers linearly (1+2+3+4 and so on), he added them in pairs, as follows: (1+100 = 101); (2+99 = 101); (3+98 = 101). He quickly realized that he had 50 pairs, each adding up to 101. This led him to the solution: 50 × 101 = 5050. That little kid turned out to be one of the greatest mathematicians that Germany (and the world) ever produced. His name was Carl Friedrich Gauss.

## What Led Gauss to Innovate?

I hope you'll all agree that Gauss approached the problem in a creative way. That much is obvious. But why was he so creative? Was it because we asked him to think outside the box or to think creatively? Obviously not! Was it because we asked him to be innovative? Again, the answer is no! What, then, led him to innovation? To answer this, we need to compare how everybody else approached the problem compared with how Gauss did it.

What the other students did was to add the numbers linearly. When that method did not help, they responded by saying (in frustration): "This problem is too difficult to solve in the time given." Like everybody else, Gauss attempted to solve the problem by adding the numbers linearly. However, when that method did not help him reach an answer, he responded by saying: "This problem is too difficult to solve in the time given *like this.*" This immediately led him to ask: "Maybe there is another way to solve it?" This, in turn, led him to start exploring other possible ways to solve the problem. In the end he got lucky: He came up with an alternative way. This is not meant to imply that every time you start searching for alternative ways to solve a problem you will find one—you may or you may not. But by starting the search, you at least give yourself the chance of discovering a solution. By contrast, the first group of students would never come up with a solution because they gave up trying.[1]

There are many things we can learn from this example. Notice, first, why the initial group gave up trying to solve the problem. They did so because they externalized the blame and in the process convinced themselves that there was nothing they could do about all the obstacles that prevented them from solving it. In other words, if you asked them why they could not solve the problem, they would answer: "Because the problem is too difficult," or "I was not given adequate resources to solve it," or "My boss never gave me a good reason why I should bother." Since they could not change any of those obstacles—they could not change the problem, or the resources available, or their boss—they lost all hope of solving the problem and so gave up. This guaranteed they would never come up with the answer. Gauss, meanwhile, did not externalize the blame. What he blamed for his inability to solve the problem was his methodology. This is liberating because the methodology you use is under your direct control. Can you do something about that? You bet! You can attempt to use a different methodology. This was exactly what Gauss did and that led him to the answer.

This is an important point and we will return to it in the next chapter. Specifically, we will explore how to get our people to focus on the things they can change rather than externalize the blame by complaining about the organization's culture, or its processes, or its (lack of) incentives. But for this chapter I want to use the Gauss example to make another crucial point: Gauss did not innovate because we asked him to innovate. He did not innovate because we asked him to think outside the box or to be creative. He innovated because he questioned his methodology. What this implies is that *innovation is not something we can ask of people*. It is, instead, a by-product of something else. That something else in this case is the active questioning of our methodologies. The idea is that if *everybody* in our organization questions our methodologies on a *continuous* basis, then innovation is likely to follow. Asking people to innovate or to "think outside the box" will not.

Questioning our methodologies is not the only behavior that leads to innovation. We know several other behaviors that are associated with innovation.[2] For example, looking beyond the narrow confines of our company or industry to get ideas from other people and organizations can be another important source of innovation. Another behavior that can lead to innovation is experimentation and trying things out without fear of failure. A classic example of this is the accidental discovery of Viagra by researchers exploring remedies for cardiovascular problems. Other behaviors that are known to lead to innovation include collaboration and working across silos; being willing to stick our neck out and assume personal responsibility for problems; thinking strategically about the business rather than focusing only on our narrow function; and working closely with both customers and non-customers to find solutions to their problems or to identify new emerging needs.

In summary, there are many behaviors that can lead to innovation and their association with innovation is well known and well established by research (see Figure 4.1). But the key point to appreciate is that innovation is a by-product of these behaviors. This means that if every single employee in an organization behaves like this on a continuous basis, then innovation will follow. Therefore, instead of asking people to innovate, we should ask them (and encourage them) to adopt these behaviors, on a daily basis.

The principle that innovation is not something we can ask of people but is something that arises if everybody in our company continuously behaves in certain ways is also applicable to the concept of *agility*. This is important for our purposes here because having created a positive sense of urgency in the organization, the next step in the process of preparing the organization for continuous transformation is to make the organization agile enough to identify and respond to whatever disruption hits us. How can we do this? Given what we have said so far, the answer should be straightforward: We will not achieve agility by asking our people to be agile. What we should do instead is to encourage everybody in the organization to adopt the day-to-day behaviors that will lead to agility. As with innovation, agility is not something we

FIGURE 4.1  What behaviors lead to innovation?

Thinking strategically about the business

Questioning our methodologies

Experimenting without fear of
failure

Working across silos

Looking for ideas outside our
company and industry

Sticking our neck out and taking
personal responsibility

Working closely with consumers
and non-consumers

Innovation

can ask of people. It is, instead, a by-product of something else—specifically, the day-to-day behaviors that will make us agile. This naturally raises two questions: What are the behaviors associated with agility, and how can we get everybody in the organization to adopt these behaviors?

## What Behaviors Lead to Agility?

To be agile, a firm must first be good at identifying changes and disruptions early, before they grow to become big threats or before the opportunity is exploited by somebody else. This implies that the *first* behavior we want to encourage in the organization is for every single employee to engage in the continuous monitoring of their local environment. As Peter Schou, former CEO of the Danish bank Lan & Spar, once told me: "How do I keep ahead of all the changes happening in my industry? Well, I have hired hundreds of spies whose job it is to keep me informed of changes happening around them." When pressed to explain what he meant by "spies," he had one word for them: "They are called employees."

This would be a radical change for most organizations.[3] Instead of being conducted once a year in a top-down way by a few employees as part of the strategy review process, monitoring should be undertaken on a continuous basis by everybody in the organization. This would imply that instead of relying on a few people to decide what information is important to collect and analyse, firms will need to switch to a decentralized, bottom-up, crowd-sourcing process. This information will be collected on a continuous basis (rather than once a year) using sophisticated management systems and AI software.

In addition to collecting information and intelligence from outside sources, internal people should be employed to provide insights and infor-mation. Knowledge about the outside environment often lies within the firm, with managers and employees being permanent observers of the busi-ness landscape. As a result, processes should be put in place to systematically and in a structured way collect data, information, and opinions about the outside environment not only from outsiders but also from insiders—both managers and employees. More importantly, this should be done on a systematic and continuous basis and not as a one-off activity.

Monitoring of the environment by everybody on a continuous basis is only the first step toward agility. The information collected is useless unless it is processed quickly and correctly to develop actionable insights. Ideally, we want this to take place in the same decentralized way by everybody in the organization. Nothing better than every single employee assuming ownership of problems arising and acting with speed to resolve them. The alternative—sending the information up the hierarchy and waiting for deci-sions to be made at the top and communicated to the rest of the organization before action can take place—is the exact opposite of what agility is all about. A good example of this principle is provided by the rapid response of the Haier Group to the COVID-19 disruption. The company was able to operate all its factories at full capacity by the end of February 2020, within two months of the start of the coronavirus crisis. A big reason for this was its decentralized organizational structure which gave a lot of autonomy to frontline leaders to adjust their own supply chains according to specialized knowledge and up-to-date information.[4]

As this example shows, giving autonomy to frontline employees to decide what disruptions they can respond to and how to respond is an effective way to increase organizational agility. However, there is a potential mine-field here. If everybody in the organization takes it upon themselves to act as they see fit, chaos and disaster may ensue. How, then, can we give autonomy without fear of losing control, or how can we do it while remaining confi-dent that the actions of every single employee aim toward the same goal?

If we think about this, parents everywhere face the same challenge with their children, especially when the children become teenagers. How can we, as parents, give our children autonomy to go out with their friends without us supervising their every step? And how can we ensure that they do not abuse the freedom and autonomy we give them by doing something stupid in our absence? The answer, of course, is by establishing a few clear parameters of what they can do and what they cannot do. As long as the decision they have to make falls within these parameters, they are free to make it without asking us. However, if the decision falls outside these parameters, they have to ask for permission.

The same principle should be applied inside an organization. When employees have to decide whether it is their responsibility to respond to a disruption or whether they should report the disruption to top management for further examination and analysis, these parameters should act as their guide. Decisions and actions that fall within these parameters can be undertaken with autonomy; actions that fall outside these parameters need to be approved by top management first. For example, deciding to respond to a competitor's move by getting closer to our customers and offering them better service should be something that every employee ought to feel free to do without having to ask for permission. Deciding to change the business model of the firm or developing a second business model next to the business model of the core business is not.

This, of course, raises the question: "What are these parameters that guide people's decisions and actions?" Again, we can derive inspiration from how we do this with our children. At home we use two types of parameters—first, we teach our children values of what is right and what is wrong; second, we set a few rules and regulations that inform them what they can do and what they cannot do. As we will argue in Chapter 6, these are the same parameters that can be used in the organization: our organization's values that can inform people what is the right thing to do; and the clear strategic choices that we have made and communicated to them to help them decide what they can do and what they cannot do. This sounds simple enough, but for values to be effective, people need to buy into them, and the sad truth is that most companies fail to "sell" their values to employees to get their buy-in, as we do with our children. As a result, instead of being the lighthouse that guides people's day-to-day behaviors, these values end up as decoration on company walls that nobody pays attention to. Even worse, most companies fail to make the difficult choices that strategy requires, and even when they do, they fail to articulate them clearly to their people. As a result, strategy remains a mystery to the very people it is supposed to be guiding—the employees. This is a topic that we will pick up again in Chapter 6 when we explore how to develop a clear strategy and communicate it effectively to the organization.

## More Behaviors for Agility

Having decided what types of problems or disruptions they should report to top management and what type of disruptions they can deal with on their own, employees need to act quickly in resolving the problems that fall within their sphere of responsibility. The problem is that what needs to be done in response to the trends, changes, and disruption identified is often not obvious or clear. Analysis paralysis and indecision may follow unless we find a way to assess quickly whether an idea is worth pursuing or not. The best way to do this is through experimentation. As long as these experiments are small-scale and low-cost ones, experimentation can speed up our response and help us learn new things in the process. The guiding principle should be "fail early, fail often" to quickly assess an idea and move forward.

A good example of this is provided by Hans Monderman, the Dutch traffic engineer who is credited with revolutionizing our thinking on road design and safety. Imagine having a road or intersection in your town where too many accidents take place. What would you do to improve driving behaviors and reduce the number of accidents? Most people facing such a task will immediately think of putting in place more traffic lights or traffic signs, or more police to monitor the area. But not Hans Monderman. He came up with the concept of the "naked street" based on the principle that the *removal* of all the things that are supposed to make a road safe—such as traffic lights, road markings, and road signs—would actually make it safer. In their place, he suggested the introduction of an open and even space that pedestrians and drivers were supposed to "share." He also advised the use of art to signal traffic flow—for example, the height of water fountains can be used to indicate how congested an intersection is. Instead of raised curbs, he recommended the use of different texture and color to denote sidewalks. He also recommended the use of lights to illuminate not only the roadbed but also the pedestrian areas. He suggested extending cafes to the edge of the street to further reinforce the idea of shared space. And he proposed the removal of all street signs, encouraging people to negotiate right of way by human interaction and eye contact.

He argued tirelessly for more than 20 years in favor of such "naked" roads as safer alternatives to roads full of signs and markings. He often complained that road design in the western world was based on the (mistaken) belief that driving and walking were utterly incompatible modes of transport and that the two should be segregated as much as possible. This led our traffic engineers to design wide roads slicing through residential areas, dividing neighborhoods, discouraging pedestrian activity, and destroying the human scale of the urban environment. Road signs proliferated and became the primary way to enforce behavior. Monderman considered this counterproductive and argued for a change in policy. Think about the ideas he proposed. If you had been his boss, how would you have reacted to them? It's hard to think of anybody who would not consider them crazy. Predictably, his arguments fell on deaf ears and his ideas received the expected resistance from his fellow engineers.

To prove his idea, he undertook a series of experiments where he reconstructed roads by making them narrower and by removing traffic lights and signs. In a famous experiment, he totally redesigned a roundabout (traffic circle) in the town of Drachten, Netherlands by removing all traffic signs, eliminating curbs, and installing art. The result was that traffic accidents all but disappeared. In another experiment in West Palm Beach, Florida, the roads were made smaller and narrower. As a result, traffic slowed so much that people felt safe to walk there. This led to an increase in pedestrian traffic that attracted new shops and apartment buildings. Property values doubled. Successes such as these turned the tide of public opinion on Monderman. Initially vilified as a dangerous maverick, he soon became a traffic engineer "pioneer." More than 100 shared space schemes have been introduced in his native Friesland, and in Groningen and Drenthe provinces, and his ideas have been implemented in several European countries as well as in the USA, Canada, Russia, South Africa, Australia, Japan, and Brazil.

It is easy to be carried away by the ideas, but lest we forget, all Monderman's ideas were driven by an underlying strong belief—that traditional tools used by traffic engineers to influence driver behavior (such as traffic lights, road signs, and road markings) are not only ineffective but downright dangerous. He strongly believed that road signs lull motorists into a false sense of security and remove all feeling of personal responsibility on the part of drivers. Instead of signs, he believed that the architecture or design of the road should be such to encourage people to behave in the right way. As he put it: "You can't expect traffic lights and street markings to encourage [the right behaviors]. You have to build it into the design of the road."[5]

There is no question that asking and encouraging frontline employees to engage in experimentation will improve our agility in the face of disruption.

FIGURE 4.2  What behaviors lead to agility?

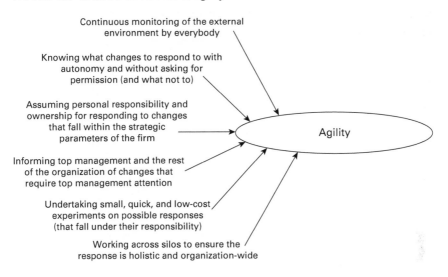

It will allow us to test quickly whether an idea works or not. It will also allow us to collect data that can be used to convince the organization of the attractiveness of the idea. This would save us from the endless debates and arguments needed to convince the rest of the organization to stop resisting the idea and get on board. It will, finally, allow us to learn new and unexpected things about our response and how to do it better. This learning will be greatly enhanced if employees "speak the same language" across the organization. One way to achieve this is by encouraging collaboration and exchange across functions and geographies. Working across silos is, therefore, another behavior that can help us become more agile.

In short, there are numerous day-to-day behaviors that are associated with agility (see Figure 4.2). The important thing is to get everybody in the organization to adopt these behaviors. This is easier said than done and we turn to this topic next.

## How Can We Get These Behaviors From Everybody?

It is one thing to make a list of behaviors we want in the organization and another to get them. In fact, the evidence is that employees rarely behave in the wonderful ways we have just described. They do not do so even when we clearly communicate to them the behaviors we want and expect of them.

There is no better example of this issue—of people *not* doing the things they know they should do—than the following.[6] On May 30, 2008 a terrible hit-and-run incident was captured on CCTV in Hartford, Connecticut. It showed 78-year-old Angel Arce Torres crossing a two-way street when he was hit by a speeding Honda. The amazing thing (captured on the video) was that nobody bothered to dash to his help or even stop the traffic as he lay motionless in the street. Several cars passed by him without stopping while a few people stared from the sidewalk. Some approached Torres, but most stayed put until a police cruiser responding to an unrelated call arrived on the scene. The incident provoked an outcry in the press and the Hartford chief of police was quoted as saying that the lack of action on the part of passersby showed that the nation had lost its moral compass. "At the end of the day we've got to look at ourselves and understand that our moral values have now changed," police chief Daryl Roberts said. "We have no regard for each other."[7]

It is interesting to note that police were blaming our "changed" moral values for this state of affairs as if an incident such as this could not have happened half a century ago (because, presumably, we had stronger moral values then). Yet, a very similar incident took place half a century ago. It happened in New York City in 1964 and involved a 29-year-old woman named Kitty Genovese.

Genovese had driven home from her job as a bar manager late on the night of March 13, 1964. She parked her car about 100 feet (30 m) from her apartment door, which was around the rear of the building. As she walked to her apartment, she was attacked by a man who stabbed her twice in the back. Her cries for help were heard by several (sleeping) neighbors and at least one of them shouted at the man to "leave that girl alone." When the attacker ran away, Genovese was able to slowly make her way to the back entrance of her apartment building where she collapsed. The attacker returned 10 minutes later and found her lying seriously injured in the hall-way at the back of the building where a locked doorway had prevented her from entering the building. He proceeded to kill her.

The murder caused a sensation because a *New York Times* article published two weeks after the murder claimed that several people had heard or observed portions of the attack, yet nobody did anything to help.[8] According to the *Times*' story, 37 people witnessed this murder but did nothing. Police later revealed that the figure was most probably 12 people, and none saw or was aware of the whole incident. Many claimed to have heard the cries but were not aware that a homicide was in progress. Although the initial perception (that many people had observed this murder and still chose to do nothing) is probably inaccurate, the fact remains that few of the people who did hear the cries called the police and nobody went downstairs to investigate or to offer help.

These are arguably extreme examples, but the problem they highlight—people *not* doing what they know they should do—is widespread in organizations. For example, we argued that employees should monitor the outside environment on a continuous basis and decide on their own what problems to report to top management and what problems to tackle themselves. This sounds like an excellent idea, but how many people actually do it? The answer is, not many. A classic example of this was revealed during the COVID-19 crisis in 2020 in China.[9] After the SARS contagion in 2002, China created a reporting system to collect information about disease quickly and easily from villages and local authorities. The aim was to then disseminate this information to regional and national authorities for quick action. It was a good idea, yet it failed during the COVID-19 crisis because local officials did not report problems for fear of being blacklisted as the bearers of bad news. Similarly, we argued that employees should take ownership of problems and should be willing to stick their neck out. Again, this is an excellent idea, but how many people do this? Yes, you guessed it, the answer is again not many. For example, academic studies of online communities have reported that almost 90 percent of members tend to social loaf—that is, to avoid taking responsibility and assume that "somebody else will do it." These are not isolated examples. There is overwhelming evidence that people do not do what they know they should do, a problem that has come to be known as "the knowing–doing gap."[10]

## The Underlying Organizational Environment Is Key

What explains this problem? For example, why did nobody come to the rescue of Kitty Genovese or Angel Arce Torres even though we all know that the right thing to do is to try to help? As noted above, some people have pointed the finger at the erosion of moral values in our society. Others have claimed that our culture is to blame for encouraging individualistic behaviors and the pursuit of personal benefit with little concern for the commons. Yet others have argued that the problem lies in the time pressures that we all face, something that shifts our priorities. Even the underlying incentives have come under criticism: Some people have argued that we may not stop to help because we are afraid that we may get in trouble by doing so. After all, we have all heard of the case of the man who rushed into a burning house to save a woman, only to be sued by that woman for damaging her spine while trying to get her out of the house.

There are three key points to note from this. The first is that it was not knowledge that produced the behaviors but a collection of other factors. In other words, people did not rush to help Kitty Genovese or Angel Arce Torres *not* because they did not know they should do so. They did, but some other factors intervened to stop them from doing what they knew they should do. The same is true inside our organization. If our employees are not following the wonderful behaviors associated with agility that we described above, the reason is not that they do not know they should do so. They do, but some factors inside the organization are preventing them from doing so. This implies that to correct suboptimal behaviors, we must first change the underlying factors that produced them. There is no sense telling people what to do if the underlying factors do not support what we are asking for. Failure to "correct" the underlying factors will lead us to the same suboptimal behaviors again and again no matter how much regulation we put in place or how much we change the people who produced the suboptimal behaviors in the first place. Numerous academic studies have found support for this position. For example, we have several celebrated experiments in the social psychology field—such as the Stanford prison experiment or Milgram's electricity experiment—that showed that the collection of these factors can have a bigger influence on how people behave than do our own personality or moral values.[11]

The second point to note is that there are several factors that produced the suboptimal behavior, such as incentives, time pressures, the underlying moral values, groupthink, diffusion of responsibility, fear of excessive responsibility, and so on. Incentives are important but they are only one of these factors. This is important to point out because economists have always taken incentives to be the primary factor driving human behaviors and have used incentives to explain all kinds of behaviors—including cheating on school exams by teachers and suboptimal actions by soccer goalkeepers facing penalty kicks.[12] There is no question that incentives are important, but they are not the only factor driving behaviors, and it's questionable whether they are even the most important factor. This implies that fiddling with the incentives alone will not be enough to change how people behave. *All* the underlying factors—or at least a lot of them—would have to be influenced if we are to change the behaviors that they produce.

The third and final point to note is that all these factors are interconnected. This is important because it means that if we try to fix one of them, we may cause a change in another and this can produce a series of unintended consequences down the road. This would make the problem even worse. Unfortunately, this problem arises far too many times in organizations because we have a tendency to address problems through linear thinking: Once a problem arises, we look for the most obvious reasons for it and address those. This almost never works because our actions affect other less obvious factors and this sets in motion a series of unintended consequences. A good example of this is provided by the actions of the state of Oregon to solve its meth problem. As described by a local newspaper in 2007,[13] "Oregon adopted the most stringent anti-meth laws in the nation – eliminating key ingredients and kick-starting a national, even global war on what many consider the most addictive and disturbing illegal narcotic. Today, it's undeniable that Oregon's laws were hugely successful in one area: The meth labs that endangered children and created hidden toxic waste dumps in basements and backyards across the state have been all but eliminated." Despite this success, the article comments further that "[police] officers indicate, however, that success has borne unintended consequences"[14] and due to a "massive influx of meth supplied by Mexican drug cartels,"[15] the meth economy has sifted over to "superlabs," which can be found in southern California and Mexico, which has ultimately made the cops' jobs harder. All this suggests that sorting out the most obvious sources to a problem is never the answer. The solution requires us to stop thinking in linear ways and to search for solutions to the problem away from its immediate and most obvious sources.

Having argued that it is the collection of several interconnected and inter-related factors that produces behaviors, the question that arises is what to call this collection of factors. In the field of social psychology, they have come to be known as the underlying "situation" or "context" in which people are placed. In the field of system dynamics, they are called the "underlying structure of a system." For our purposes here, we will call them the underlying "organizational environment."

Fully appreciating that it is the underlying organizational environment that is primarily responsible for the behaviors we observe in the organization is one of the most profound principles in management. Though simple, we are often reluctant to apply it in how we manage people. As a result, the moment something goes wrong, we search for scapegoats in people. We have this inbuilt belief that if someone did something wrong, this individual needs to be punished for it. We rarely look to rectify the underlying organizational environment that encouraged that individual to misbehave. For example, consider the following statement by Charles Ferguson, the director of the movie *Inside Job*, while accepting the 2010 Oscar for Best Documentary.[16] "Three years after a horrific financial crisis caused by massive fraud, not a single financial executive has gone to jail." This is a classic example of blaming people for bad behavior without paying enough attention to the underlying reasons that led them to the bad behavior in the first place. The sad truth is that if the underlying reasons are not corrected, the same bad behaviors will emerge again and again no matter how many people you punish or how severe the punishment. The same bias manifests itself in our attempts to improve behaviors in an organization by removing the "bad apples" and replacing them with "better" people. This almost always fails. It doesn't matter how "good" the new people are. If you put them in the same organizational environment, you will soon get the same bad behaviors out of them as you did with "bad" people.

Turning now to the issue at the heart of this chapter—how to get every single employee in our organization to adopt the wonderful behaviors of agility that we identified earlier—the answer should be obvious. The only way to get our people behaving like that is by creating around them an organizational environment that supports and promotes these behaviors. If the existing organizational environment does not produce the desired behaviors, we need to change it. Such a task may sound like a tall order, but as Jay Forrester commented: "All [social systems] seem to have a few sensitive influence points through which the behavior of the system can be changed."[17] We will explore this topic in the next chapter.

## What Is the Organizational Environment?

So far, we have defined the organizational environment as the collection of interconnected factors that determine how people behave in that environment. It will help if we are a bit more specific about these factors. There are obviously many factors that make up the organizational environment, but the major ones that we will consider here are four: first is the *culture* that exists in the organization which includes its norms, values, and unquestioned assumptions; second are the *structures and processes* of the organization, comprising not only its formal hierarchy but also its physical set-up as well as its systems (information, recruitment, market research, and the like); third are the positive or negative *incentives* in the organization, both monetary and non-monetary ones; and finally is the *people* we hire, bringing with them their own mindsets, attitudes, and assumptions. It is the combination of these four elements that creates the underlying organizational environment, which in turn produces behaviors that either create or solve a problem. This is shown in Figure 4.3.

A good example of how the organizational environment determines behaviors is provided by the Swedish music and video streaming company Spotify.[18] The company has adopted a unique organizational structure that is made up of numerous autonomous units of no more than eight people. These units are called squads and depending on what products or technologies they are working on, are grouped into bigger units called tribes. The tribes themselves are linked through chapters that serve like a corporate center for the squads. Each chapter has a formal leader who is also a squad member and whose primary role is to act as a coach to the squads. Individual squad members can switch squads while maintaining their formal tribe leader. The small size of the squads encourages speedy decision making as well as face-to-face interactions and personal relationships. The culture created is friendly and supportive. It will come as no surprise to know that in such an environment, the behaviors of collaboration and agility are widespread and followed by all employees.

FIGURE 4.3  What is the organizational environment?

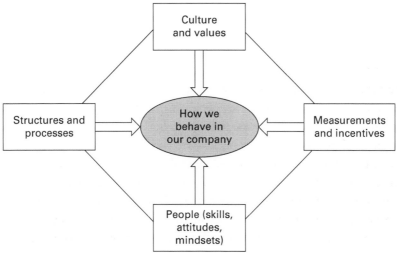

Consider also the company E. Leclerc, France's biggest food retailer by market share which boasts revenues of €38 billion a year.[19] It is hard to differentiate yourself if you are a supermarket, but Leclerc has built a unique organizational environment that allows its people to be agile entrepreneurs while being part of a huge company. The organizational structure of Leclerc is the first element of its environment that promotes the behaviors of agility, innovation, and entrepreneurship: The company is not a single company but a federation of entrepreneurs, each owning their own store. They are allowed to trade under the Leclerc name as long as they abide by certain norms and regulations—the primary ones being that they will be the cheapest store in their area and that they cannot own more than two stores. Each store has total autonomy over its affairs, but they also coordinate with central office in Paris and can take advantage of Leclerc's regional warehouses to buy bulk. They can rely on the company's central purchasing department to negotiate prices and select suppliers. The company's culture is the second element in its environment that promotes initiative-taking and psychological safety. The company boasts a strong family culture where everybody is treated with fairness and openness and where everybody is equal. Store owners contribute to the running of the organization by attending monthly regional meetings as well as frequent national meetings where information is exchanged and key strategic decisions are taken. The culture is sustained by the fact that new Leclerc stores are always started by current Leclerc employees, who receive the financial backing and guarantees of current Leclerc store owners.

There are more elements to the Leclerc organizational environment that we could point to. For example, the organization is united by a common and deeply felt vision that the company is not just selling food products but also changing French society and correcting unfair practices in the system. The company's incentive systems are also quite unique—every store owner must distribute 25 percent of the store's profits to its employees at the end of every year. But the overall message I want to convey is that it is the combination of all these things that makes up the organizational environment and that it is this environment that, in turn, determines to a large extent how people behave on a day-to-day basis. This suggests that to get the behaviors of agility that we identified earlier in this chapter, we must first put in place an organizational environment that supports these behaviors. This raises the question: "How can we develop such a supporting organizational environment?" We turn to this topic next.

# References

**1**  We do not know for sure how Gauss came up with the answer to this problem. The account presented here is one of many possibilities. For a comprehensive treatment of this topic see Brian Hayes: "Gauss's day of reckoning," *American Scientist*, May–June 2006, Vol. 94, pp. 200–205.

**2**  Gary Pisano: "The hard truth about innovative cultures," *Harvard Business Review*, January–February 2019, pp. 62–71.

**3**  Constantinos Markides, Daniel Oyon, Mael Schnegg, and Tony Davila: "Firms need new ways to monitor their environment," *Think at London Business School*, August 12, 2019.

**4**  Howard Yu and Mark Greeven: "How autonomy creates resilience in the face of crisis," *MIT Sloan Management Review*, March 23, 2020.

**5**  Tom McNichol: "Roads gone wild," *Wired*, December 12, 2004, Issue 12.

**6**  The section that follows and the one after it were originally published as: Costas Markides and Anita McGahan: "Achieving change that lasts," *Think at London Business School* (formerly *London Business School Review*) © London Business School 2015. Reprinted with permission.

**7**  "Connecticut hit-and-run: Where have all the Samaritans gone?" *The Guardian*, June 5, 2008.

**8**  "37 who saw murder didn't call the police," *The New York Times*, March 27, 1964, p. 1.

**9**  Steve Lee Myers: "China created a fail-safe system to track contagions. It failed," *The New York Times*, March 29, 2020.

**10**  Jeffrey Pfeffer and Robert Sutton: *The Knowing–Doing Gap: How smart companies turn knowledge into action*, Boston, MA: Harvard Business Review Press, 1999.

**11**  Lee Ross and Richard E. Nisbett: *The Person and the Situation: Perspectives of social psychology*, New York: McGraw-Hill, 1991.

**12**  Steven Levitt and Stephen Dubner: *Freakonomics*, New York: William Morrow, 2005; S. Levitt and S. Dubner: *Think Like a Freak*, New York: William Morrow, 2014.

**13**  Nick Budnick: "One meth problem leads to another," *The West Linn Tidings*, November 29, 2007, updated October 30, 2009.

**14**  Ibid.

**15**  Ibid.

**16**  *TIME*, March 14, 2011, p. 15.

**17**  Jay W. Forrester: *The Collected Papers of Jay W. Forrester* (Chapter 14, p. 220), Cambridge, MA: Wright-Allen Press, 1975.

**18**  Michael Mankins and Eric Garton: "How Spotify balances employee autonomy and accountability," *Harvard Business Review*, February 9, 2017.

**19**  A lengthier account of Leclerc can be found in my book: Costas Markides: *All the Right Moves: A guide to crafting breakthrough strategy*, Boston, MA: Harvard Business School Press, 2000, pp. 109–111.

# 05

# Develop a Supporting Organizational Environment in a Decentralized Way

Creating the organizational environment that supports and promotes the behaviors of agility—as articulated in the previous chapter—does not necessarily have to be done in a centralized way and does not have to be undertaken by top management alone. Individual managers and team leaders scattered all over the organization can achieve major changes in their local organizational environments through a few small and targeted actions. Done within prescribed parameters as set by top management, these *decentralized* actions could start a thousand little fires that can grow into an inferno that transforms the organizational environment of the whole company.

To appreciate this point, consider the story of David Kennedy. You probably never heard of him, but he is considered a pioneer and a radical thinker who is revolutionizing the way we deal with drugs in the inner cities. Kennedy is really an unlikely candidate for this—he does not have a degree in criminology, nor did he ever study crime prevention. Instead, he studied philosophy at Swarthmore. Yet, he is credited as the only person to come up with a consistently viable and cost-effective strategy for helping inner cities deal with the problem of drugs.[1] What is his big idea? Simple—you cannot solve this problem without getting the local community to help. And to get the local community to help, you have to earn their trust. To achieve this, you have to demonstrate to them through actions (and over time) that you really want to help them and that you have their interests at heart. Thus, rather than go after young drug dealers with the intention of arresting them, how about helping them to get out of drugs?

In a 2004 experiment in High Point, North Carolina, Kennedy got the police to round up young drug dealers and showed them videos of them dealing drugs. The police told them that they had prepared cases against them and were all set for indictment. But instead of proceeding with indictment, they let these young dope dealers go back home. They then worked with their families to help them get training and new jobs. The message, which spread quickly through the neighborhood, was that the cops were not out for arrests. Instead, they really wanted to help by giving kids a second chance—but they would get aggressive if they didn't take that chance. Over time, the police won the local community's trust and cooperation. The kids themselves began pointing out the big drug dealers in the area and this led to their arrest. According to *Newsweek*: "After four years, police in High Point had wiped the drug dealers off the corner. They compared the numbers to the prior four years and found a 57 percent drop in violent crime in the targeted area."[2]

Kennedy's tactics are now being adopted by police departments all over the US. Although the strategy is not without its critics—who see this as being "soft" on criminals—police departments across the nation are reporting impressive results from his "good-cop" approach. This story highlights a key point I want to make in this chapter: Small changes can have a big impact.[3] What Kennedy did is not radical or revolutionary. It does not require major investments or huge amounts of resources. It is something that can be done quickly and by few people, even an individual. Yet look at the enormous impact it had! This is the principle made popular by Thaler and Sunstein's book *Nudge* and it is the principle that I will use in this chapter to build the case that we can create the organizational environment that supports and promotes the behaviors of agility in a decentralized way.

## Small Changes, Big Impact

The story of David Kennedy is not an isolated one. There are many examples that demonstrate the principle that small changes can have a big impact.[4] For example, thousands of people die every year waiting for a suitable donor organ. Encouraging people to donate their organs after death is, therefore, a matter of life and death for many patients. Some countries are better at this than others. According to a 1993 Gallup poll, 28 percent of Americans granted permission by signing a donor card.[5] As Table 5.1 shows, this is much higher than the consent rate in countries such as Denmark, Germany, and the UK but much lower than in countries such as Austria, Hungary, and France.[6]

TABLE 5.1  Percent of people in each country who are organ donors

| Country | Effective consent rate (%) |
|---------|---------------------------|
| Denmark | 4.2 |
| Germany | 12 |
| United Kingdom | 17.2 |
| Netherlands | 27.5 |
| Sweden | 86 |
| Belgium | 98 |
| Poland | 99.5 |
| Portugal | 99.6 |
| Hungary | 100 |
| France | 100 |
| Austria | 100 |

The natural question that these statistics raise is: Why are countries like Austria and France so much better than countries such as Denmark and Germany at getting their people to donate their organs? It's hard to see culture or religion playing a role because countries that are very similar in these dimensions (such as Germany and Austria, or Denmark and Sweden) display dramatically different behaviors. It's also hard to explain it by demographic factors (such as per capita income, education levels, or life expectancy) because the European countries listed above do not differ much on these dimensions.

It turns out that the reason behind these dramatic differences is something very simple. In the low-consent countries, people are asked to fill out a form which says: "Check the box if you want to participate in the donor program." In the high-consent countries, the request is slightly different: "Check the box if you do *not* want to participate in this donor program." In both cases, most people do not, in general, check the box. But in the first case, this means that they do not become donors while in the second case it means that they become donors.

TABLE 5.2   The more people you eat with, the more food you eat

| How many people eating with you | How much more food you eat (vs eat alone) |
| --- | --- |
| 1 | 33% more |
| 2 | 47% |
| 3 | 58% |
| 4 | 69% |
| 5 | 70% |
| 6 | 72% |
| 7 | 96% |

The example obviously shows that whoever designed the questions has a dramatic influence on what we choose to do, a point made in *Nudge*. But more importantly, it shows that small differences in the questions asked/ requests made could have a big effect on the outcome. As another example of this principle, consider how much food we eat in the company of others. What would be your guess—will you expect to eat more or less food if you are eating with other people than if you are eating alone? On the face of it, you'd expect small differences—after all, your hunger should be satisfied by the same intake of food whether you eat alone or not. Yet, consider Table 5.2.[7]

Not only do we eat more when we have company but the nature of the people that eat with us could have a significant effect on our food intake. For example, women tend to eat more when they eat with a man than when eating with another woman, and we all tend to eat significantly more when eating with spouse, family, or friends.[8]

## The Butterfly Principle[9]

Both examples highlight a fundamental principle that is at the heart of this chapter: Small and seemingly trivial changes in the immediate environment or in the way we behave can have a big influence on what people do or how they behave.

This is not a new principle. In 1961, a meteorologist at MIT named Edward Lorenz constructed a mathematical model containing a set of 12 differential equations to predict weather patterns. One day, he wanted to re-examine a sequence of data coming from his model and to save time he manually entered data in the model from the printout of the previous run. To his amazement, the results from the second run were dramatically different from the results of the previous run. Upon further examination, he realized that he had entered the data to three decimal points whereas the previous run had used the same data but to six decimal points. This tiny difference in initial conditions had produced completely different results. These observations ultimately led him to formulate what we now call "the butterfly effect"—a term derived from an academic paper Lorenz presented in 1972, entitled: "Predictability: Does the flap of a butterfly's wings in Brazil set off a tornado in Texas?"

The butterfly effect has been used to explain numerous major changes in society. For example, in his wonderful book *The Tipping Point*, Malcolm Gladwell describes how William Bratton—first as head of the New York Transit Authority's police force in 1990–1994 and then as head of the New York Police Department in 1994–1996—managed to dramatically reduce crime in New York City by implementing a few (seemingly) minor changes— such as cracking down on fare beating on the subway and going after people who committed quality-of-life crimes such as public drunkenness and public urination.[10] Similarly, in their book *Nudge*, Professors Richard Thaler and Cass Sunstein describe several examples where small changes produced radical results. For example, by painting the image of a black housefly in each urinal, authorities at Amsterdam's Schiphol airport have reduced spillage in men's rooms by 80 percent. Similarly, officials in Minnesota achieved a significant increase in tax compliance by simply telling people that more than 90 percent of Minnesotans already complied in full with their tax obligations. Yet another example Thaler and Sunstein use comes from the state of Texas where authorities achieved a 29 percent reduction in roadside littering within a year of launching the "Don't Mess with Texas" advertising campaign.[11]

Equally impressive examples of the butterfly effect have been provided by social psychologists through a number of experiments.[12] For example, it has been shown that asking people to donate blood by having a friendly peer complying with the request can increase the success rate from 25 percent to 67 percent. More importantly, none of the subjects in the no-model experiment followed up the request by giving blood whereas 33 percent of the subjects in the model experiment showed up.[13] Similarly, simply commending children for already being very clean and tidy increased their tidiness by a factor of four in the short term, a behavior that remained unchanged long after the experiment was completed. Children who were told to be more tidy increased their tidiness in the short term by a factor of two but reverted to their pre-test level of littering after the experiment. Children who were neither told to be more tidy nor praised for being tidy did not change their littering behavior.[14]

Within the world of business, we also have several examples where small and apparently insignificant changes can have major impact on how people behave. For example, in the famous "Hawthorne experiments" of 1927–1932 undertaken at the Hawthorne plant of the Western Electric Company in Chicago, the productivity of assembly line employees increased by up to 30–40 percent with a change in a number of conditions, such as the frequency and duration of rest periods and meal breaks. Productivity increased whether these conditions were increased or decreased![15] In another study, workers in a pajama factory were asked to take on board a seemingly small change in the way the pajamas were sewn or boxed. One group of workers was simply informed of the change. In another group, a selected team of workers was asked to meet with management and then inform the rest of the employees about the change and help with the implementation. In yet another group, all the employees became "special operators" and were asked to help implement the change. The difference in productivity gains was dramatic. The first group experienced a sharp drop in productivity and a loss of morale (17 percent quit their job). In the second group, there was no morale loss (nobody quit their job) and the initial drop in productivity was regained within two weeks. In the third group, morale remained high and a slight drop in productivity (for one day) was soon followed by a steady increase to a level 15 percent higher than the pre-experiment level.[16]

## Decentralized Change Through Small Actions

How can we apply this principle inside our organization? In the previous chapter, we proposed that we need to put in place the organizational environment that supports and promotes the behaviors of agility. The question that immediately arises is *how* to create such an organizational environment. One way—and the method most organizations adopt—is top-down, through a major culture change program. Is this the only way to do it? The butterfly principle suggests that there is an alternative and possibly better way: Individual managers and team leaders could take it upon themselves to introduce small changes in their own *local* environments. The right kind of changes, done properly, can produce big changes in each of these local environments. If all these local changes are undertaken within an overarching framework and within strategic parameters developed by top management, then the sum of many local changes could add up to one big change in the organizational environment of the whole organization. The key point here is that individual team leaders and managers should take action only within clear parameters and guidelines set by top management, otherwise chaos might ensue. As long as individual actions fall within these parameters, the collection of these actions could add up to a big change. Many little fires could grow into an inferno that transforms the environment of the whole organization.

Academic research has identified a number of examples of "small fires" that individual leaders could light up at the local level with the aim of changing the environment in which their people operate. By far the most influential of such small changes that can be adopted is small and symbolic changes in our day-to-day behaviors. We all know that employees pay close attention to how their leaders behave and what they say. Based on what they see or hear, they form their beliefs, which tend to be reinforced and strengthened over time. The collection of these beliefs is nothing more than the culture of the organization. What this implies is simple: If culture is created through the day-to-day actions of leaders, then the way to change culture is by changing those behaviors. In doing this, leaders have an ace up their sleeves. We know that whatever leaders do or say can be magnified a hundred times by people around them. This has a serious implication: Leaders should pick one or two behaviors that they want to change in their organization and adopt those behaviors themselves. The trick is to do so in a visible and symbolic way. As if by magic, employees will soon get the message and begin to behave that way themselves.

A good example that highlights this point is the story of Nandu Nandkishore, the market head at Nestlé Philippines in 2005, who succeeded in transforming the culture of the local organization within a year. Because he wanted to encourage more collaboration among his people, the first change he introduced when he took over was a total redesign of the executive floor where he sat with his secretaries. Out went the private entrance for the market head, the security guards to his office, his private bathroom, and the offices of the secretaries that surrounded his office, preventing anybody from reaching him without their permission. In their place he created a more open floor where his (smaller) office was easily accessible by anybody and where cross-functional teams sat together. On every floor in the building, the walls were converted into glass and reduced in height from 9 feet to 3 feet to allow easier communication and interaction among people. Nandkishore also started regular townhall meetings as well as weekly market visits, and he made it his routine to walk the floor several times a day, talking and interacting with employees. It wasn't long before the whole organization got the message: Collaboration and open communication is the new game in town.

### Additional Small Changes to Undertake

Symbolically changing our behaviors is not the only thing we could attempt to change. It is also important to consider language. For example, academic research has shown that we are more likely to influence people if we emphasize their identity rather than their behavior, something that I mentioned earlier in this book.[17] What this implies is that we are more likely to encourage innovative behaviors in the organization if we tell people "be an innovator" rather than "please innovate." Similarly, we are more likely to achieve cooperative behaviors if we tell our people "be a team player" rather than "get out of your silos" or "please collaborate more." Another example of how language can be used to influence people is based on the fact that people think in relative terms. A great experiment that highlights this principle asked people to choose between $6 in cash or a good pen.[18] The majority (85 percent) chose the cash and only 15 percent chose the good pen. A second experiment gave people three options: $6 in cash, a good pen, or a bad pen. Amazingly, 55 percent chose the good pen (with 40 percent choosing the cash and 5 percent going for the bad pen). The number of people choosing the good pen went from 15 percent in the first scenario to 55 percent in the second scenario. Why? What made the good pen such an attractive alternative in the second scenario? The answer is simple: We placed it next to the bad pen and this elevated its appeal in the eyes of the participants. That people think in relative terms is a well-known fact. All we are suggesting here is that we can use this simple fact to influence our people toward the behaviors we want. How? Instead of asking people to adopt a certain behavior, X, it is better to give them a choice between two behaviors: the one we want them to adopt (X) and another one which is so unattractive that X becomes an attractive alternative.

Yet another small change to consider is what kind of issues we choose to communicate to our people based on another simple fact that we have known for years—that human beings like to conform to what others are doing. There is a lot of evidence that people like to do what other people do. A study undertaken by Professor George Land found an alarming decline in our creativity as we grow older.[19] For example, when a group of 3–5-year-old children was tested for divergent thinking (a prerequisite to creativity), about 98 percent were rated as "geniuses in creativity." The same children were tested again five years later and—alarmingly—the creativity geniuses had fallen to 32 percent of the sample. Even worse, when the same kids were tested again five years later when they were teenagers, only 12 percent were rated as geniuses in creativity. When a group of adults over the age of 25 was given the test, only 2 percent received the "genius" rating. These are the facts and they basically show that as we go through life, we learn to conform and to do what other people do. Leaders can use this fact to influence their employees. How? By "advertising" the behaviors they want to encourage in their organization. For example, advertise that the majority of your employees are team players rather than complain about those that do not collaborate as much as you want. Similarly, advertise that the majority of your people come to work on time rather than complain about those that arrive to work late. Simply "advertising" the right behavior will encourage everybody to conform to that.

It sounds simple, but the truth of the matter is that we do the exact opposite in organizations: We complain about the lack of cooperation, or people arriving late to work, or not experimenting enough. By doing this, we are advertising the "bad" behaviors and in the process encouraging even good employees to conform to them. A good example of this was provided by the "Just Say No" advertising campaign championed by the late Nancy Reagan, the president's wife, in the mid-1980s. This was an attempt to encourage high-school kids to resist peer pressure to experiment with drugs. The message was that even if many of their friends and classmates were into drugs, they should resist the pressure to do the same by saying no to drugs. The campaign failed.[20] A key reason for this was that by telling kids that they should not listen to their classmates, the campaign was in effect advertising to them that many of their peers were doing drugs. This put pressure on them to conform to what "most others" were doing. The lesson is simple: Advertise the good behaviors, not the bad ones.

Another change to consider is the incentives that we use to motivate people. Whereas all of us immediately think of money whenever the word "incentives" is used, the truth of the matter is that non-monetary incentives can be equally if not more impactful on people's behaviors, especially in organizations where creative and conceptual work is the norm.[21] Among the most important non-monetary incentives we can use are things like recognition and praise, giving people challenging tasks, giving them autonomy, and giving them access to top management time and attention. These are all incentives that are under the direct control of every individual manager and team leader, which means they can be used without permission from the top. Furthermore, unlike money, they are not in short supply.

A final change to think about is the physical environment in which your people work. Consider the 2010 study undertaken by researchers at the Harvard Medical School.[22] They analysed thousands of peer-reviewed academic papers mapping the precise location of the co-authors. They then explored whether there was any relationship between the quality of the work and how close to each other the co-authors' offices were. What they found was that when co-authors were closer together, their papers tended to be of significantly higher quality. For example, the best research was consistently produced when the co-authors were working within ten meters of each other while the lower-quality output was produced by co-authors who were located one kilometer or more away from each other. These results suggest that people will work more effectively together when they are placed in physical environments that allow or encourage frequent and physical interactions. At a time when work is becoming more virtual, companies will have to find creative ways to achieve this.

A good example that illustrates this insight is Building 20 at MIT. This was constructed in 1942 as an extension of the Radiation Laboratory to house scientists working on new technologies to aid the war effort. Hastily constructed for temporary use, Building 20 turned out to be the incubator of some of the biggest technological innovations during the Second World War, including the development of radar. What was the secret of success? According to one report, it was the close collaboration among scientists from different disciplines that was achieved primarily because of the building's unique design: "Strangely enough, the very things that made it bad also made it ideal for collaboration and innovation. Thin, wood-stud walls covered modestly by plywood allowed the engineers to manipulate the building for any need... Furthermore, the building was notoriously hard to navigate. This would often lead occupants astray into different offices and laboratories and provide chance opportunities for intellectual discussion. These informal hallway discussions would often lead to cross-departmental collaboration on new projects."[23]

Another example of the same principle is provided by Steve Jobs' insistence that the campus of Pixar had to be designed in a way that facilitated interactions among employees. According to one report: "[Steve Jobs] designed the building to make people get out of their offices and mingle in the central atrium with people they might not otherwise see." The atrium "was planned by Jobs to house the campus' only restrooms. The idea was that people who naturally isolate themselves would be forced to have great conversations, even if that took place while washing their hands."[24]

## Some Small Actions Are More Impactful Than Others

These are just a few examples of the "small" things that individual managers or team leaders could undertake to improve the local organizational environment in which their people operate. There are many more. The important thing is to allow each manager to use their creativity to come up with actions that fit their management style and the company culture. Of course, not all small changes will result in big changes. Surely we should not expect that small changes in everything will produce the desired effects! An analogy can help make the point. If you place a grain of sand on a beach, nothing will happen. However, if you place a grain of sand at the tip of a big pyramid made of sand, that little extra weight may cause the whole pyramid to collapse. This is what we are looking for—little grains of sand that can cause the collapse of the pyramid. The question is: "What are these grains of sand in an organization?"

The answer is to identify what academics in the system dynamics field call "high-leverage" points in the system. As Jay Forrester, the founding father of this academic discipline, commented: "All [systems] seem to have a few sensitive influence points through which the behavior of the system can be changed."[25] The trick is therefore to find what the high-leverage points in a given system or company are. Different companies have different leverage points. It is also impossible to really identify them ex ante. They become evident only after the fact. This implies that we should cast as wide a net as possible in the "small" actions we undertake in the organization. The more small actions we undertake, the higher the probability that one or two of them will turn out to be high leverage points in the system.

The decentralized approach to changing the organizational environment advocated in this chapter cannot succeed unless clear parameters are put in place to guide individual managers and team leaders in what they can do and what they cannot do without top management approval. This is an issue that we raised in the last chapter as well. Yes, individual employees should be given autonomy to respond to changes and disruptions because doing so will enhance our agility and speed of response; however, autonomy without some constraints or guiding parameters can lead to chaos. It is therefore imperative that people know what these guiding parameters are. We turn to this topic next.

## References

1   Suzanne Smalley: "Always on my mind," *Newsweek*, January 31, 2009.

2   Ibid.

3   This is the principle underpinning the work of Richard Thaler and Cass Sunstein: *Nudge: Improving decisions about health, wealth and happiness*, London: Penguin Books, 2009.

4   The ideas presented in this section were originally published as: Costas Markides and Anita McGahan: "What if small changes really could change the world?" *Think at London Business School* (formerly *London Business School Review*) © London Business School 2015. Reprinted with permission.

5   The Gallup Organization: "The American public's attitude toward organ donation and transplantation," Gallup Organization, Princeton, NJ, 1993.

6   Eric J. Johnson and Daniel Goldstein: "Do defaults save lives?" *Science*, November 2003, Vol. 302, No. 21, pp. 1338–1339.

7   John M. de Castro: "Eating behavior: Lessons from the real world of humans," *Nutrition*, 2000, Vol. 16, No. 10, pp. 800–813.

8   Ibid, p. 804.

9   The ideas presented in this section were originally published as: Costas Markides and Anita McGahan: "What if small changes really could change the world?" *Think at London Business School* (formerly *London Business School Review*) © London Business School 2015. Reprinted with permission.

10   In the period 1992–1997, murders in NYC declined by 64 percent and total crimes declined by 50 percent. See Malcolm Gladwell: *The Tipping Point*, New York: Little, Brown and Company, 2000, pp. 5–6.

11   All examples come from Richard Thaler and Cass Sunstein: *Nudge: Improving decisions about health, wealth and happiness*, London: Penguin Books, 2009.

**12**  An excellent book that provides a summary of experiments in social psychology is Lee Ross and Richard E. Nisbett: *The Person and the Situation: Perspectives of social psychology*, Boston, MA: McGraw-Hill, 1991.

**13**  J. Philippe Rushton and Anne C. Campbell: "Modeling, vicarious reinforcement and extroversion on blood donating in adults: Immediate and long-term effects," *European Journal of Social Psychology*, 1977, Vol. 7, pp. 297–306.

**14**  Richard Miller, Phillip Brickman, and Diana Bolen: "Attribution versus persuasion as a means of modifying behavior," *Journal of Personality and Social Psychology*, 1975, Vol. 3, pp. 430–441.

**15**  Although the Hawthorne studies have now been criticized for methodological flaws, nobody disputes the fact that dramatic increases in worker productivity were achieved. The methodological flaws make it more difficult to explain why. See note 12, Ross and Nisbett, pp. 210–212.

**16**  Lester Coch and John French Jr: "Overcoming resistance to change," *Human Relations*, 1948, Vol. 1, pp. 512–532.

**17**  Christopher Bryan, Gabrielle Adams, and Benoit Monin: "When cheating would make you a cheater: Implicating the self prevents unethical behaviour," *Journal of Experimental Psychology: General*, 2013, Vol. 142, No. 4, pp. 1001–1005.

**18**  Itamar Simonson and Amos Tversky: "Choice in context: Tradeoff contrast and extremeness aversion," *Journal of Marketing Research*, 1992, Vol. 29, No. 3, pp. 281–295.

**19**  George Land and Beth Jarman: *Breakpoint and Beyond: Mastering the future today*, New York: HarperBusiness, 1992.

**20**  Scott Lilienfeld and Hal Arkowitz: "Why 'Just say no' doesn't work," *Scientific America*, January 1, 2014.

**21**  Daniel Pink: *Drive: The surprising truth about what motivates us*, New York: Riverhead Books, 2009.

**22**  Kyungjoo Lee, John Brownstein, Richard Mills, and Isaac Kohane: "Does collocation inform the impact of collaboration?" *PLoS ONE*, December 15, 2010.

**23**  David Shaffer: "Building 20: What made it so special and why it will (probably) never exist again," *DJC Oregon*, June 19, 2012.

**24**  "Pixar headquarters and the legacy of Steve Jobs," *Office Snapshots.com*, July 16, 2012.

**25**  Jay W. Forrester: *The Collected Papers of Jay W. Forrester*, Chapter 14, p. 220, Cambridge, MA: Wright-Allen Press, 1975.

# 06

# How to Give Autonomy
# Without Losing Control

The last chapter made the point that we can change the firm's organizational environment in a decentralized way. We can do this by giving autonomy to individual managers and team leaders to introduce *small* changes in their own *local* environment. The sum of these local changes can result in a major change in the overall organizational environment. This sounds like a much better way to change the firm's organizational environment than the centralized, top-down approach followed by most firms. However, the decentralized approach is not risk free. What happens if the individual actions do not add up to one coherent change? Is the decentralized approach proposed here a recipe for bottom-up change or a recipe for chaos, with the organization moving in a hundred different directions?

These are important questions for us to answer because many of the things we have proposed in this book so far depend on people operating with autonomy. For example, we proposed in Chapter 4 that our responsiveness to disruptions will be enhanced if frontline employees are allowed to monitor the outside environment on a continuous basis and then decide what changes to report to top management and what changes to respond to on their own and in what way. Similarly, we proposed in Chapter 5 that the best way to change the firm's organizational environment is by giving individual managers and team leaders the freedom to undertake small changes in their respective local organizational environments, the collection of which will change the environment of the whole firm. How can we make sure that all this autonomy and initiative taking all over the organization does not end up in disaster?

When I asked the managing partner of a US-based multinational brokerage firm this question, his reply was the following: "I give my people the canvas and the paint. It's up to them to decide what they paint and how." What he meant by this was that his people can have autonomy, but within certain boundaries: Yes, they can paint whatever they want, but it has to be on our canvas, using only the paint that we give them. A similar analogy was given to me by the CEO of a French supermarket chain: "I tell my people where I want them to be and by what time. It is their decision how to get there." Both of these responses suggest that the generic answer to the question we are asking is simple enough: You can give people autonomy, but it has to be within certain parameters or boundaries. These parameters will guide our people— when the decision they have to make falls within these parameters, they will have autonomy to make it; if, however, the decision they have to make falls outside these parameters, they will not have autonomy to make it but will have to ask permission or advice from senior management.

Few people would disagree with this principle, but the devil is always in the detail. Specifically, what exactly are these parameters? And what exactly is the difference between parameters that guide behaviors versus initiative-killing rules and regulations? I will explore these questions in this chapter. Specifically, I will propose that there are two types of parameters that the organization needs to put in place. The first is the organization's clearly communicated strategy. This is nothing more than the difficult strategic choices we have made that determine what decisions are "strategic" (and should be undertaken only by top management) and what decisions are "operational" and can be undertaken by employees. The second parameter that we will explore is the organization's values and purpose. As long as these are ingrained in the organization's DNA, they will help employees decide what actions support our purpose and values and what actions do not support them. This, in turn, will help them decide what to do themselves and what to refer to senior management to decide. There is nothing surprising in the two types of parameters that I am proposing here, but the problem is that organizations consistently and predictably mess up the implementation of both.

## Parameter #1: Clear Strategy Choices[1]

Decisions about strategy are the prerogative of top management and cannot be delegated to employees. For example, deciding what customers to target or what products to sell are strategic decisions and must be made by top management. Similarly, changes to strategy are also the domain of top management. You cannot have employees changing the product offering or the customers being targeted without the direct input of their leaders. Feedback from the market is obviously important and cannot be ignored. If this feedback is about the need to change or adjust the strategy, then employees must report it to their managers for them to decide. If the feedback is about operational issues, then employees can respond to it with autonomy. The principle is, therefore, simple enough: Employees can have autonomy to act on operational issues that improve what we are already doing, but not on the strategic choices that the organization has made that define its strategic direction.

Obviously, for employees to tell the difference between operational and strategic issues, they must first know what strategic choices the organization has made. This implies that the most important parameter that will guide employees' behaviors—and the parameter that will allow us to give autonomy without fear of losing control—is our clearly communicated strategy. By this, I mean the difficult choices the organization has made on three key issues: *who* to target as customers and who not to target; *what* to offer these customers and what not to offer; and *how* to play the game relative to competitors—that is, what value chain activities to adopt and what not to adopt. This sounds simple enough, but there is overwhelming evidence that shows that employees in most companies do not know the strategic choices their company has made. For example, a 2013 academic study reported that even in high-performing companies with clearly articulated strategies, only 29 percent of employees knew what their company's strategy was.[2] This is not an isolated finding—survey after survey reports that employees seem to be in the dark when it comes to their organization's strategy, despite claims by senior management that their strategy is clear, well communicated, and understood by their employees.[3]

This surely is a mystery! Organizations spend huge amounts of resources (time, money, attention, and energy) to develop their strategies. They spend equally impressive amounts of time and energy communicating their strategies to the rest of the organization. Why is it that most of these employees claim to have no knowledge of these strategies? There are obviously many reasons for such an unfortunate state of affairs—a difficult-to-explain strategy perhaps, or maybe insufficient (or bad) communication by top management, or perhaps passive listening or lack of attention by the employees. However, I want to single out three specific reasons for this lack of clarity in strategy.

### Reason #1: Failure to Make the Difficult Choices That Strategy Requires

Strategy is all about making difficult choices—what the organization will do, and more importantly, what it will *not* do. The question that immediately arises is: "choices about what?" There is no agreed answer to this question, but at the very least there are three choices about strategy that need to be made—the *who*, the *what*, and the *how*. Specifically:

- Who should we target as customers and who should we not?
- What shall we offer these customers and what shall we not?
- How should we achieve all this—what value chain activities should we undertake and what activities should we not?

The choices that we make on these three parameters constitute the organization's strategy. They define its position in the industry and they act as the boundaries within which our people can act with freedom and autonomy. I have written elsewhere *how* to make these choices and *who* is responsible for making them.[4] The usual question that people ask when presented with this simple point is whether these three choices are the only choices that an organization needs to make in developing its strategy. How about the *where*, the *why*, and the *when*, people often ask? Wouldn't our strategy be incomplete if we do not make choices on these additional issues? Valid as this question might be, it still misses the point. The real problem that most organizations face is not whether they need to make three or four or five choices but how to get their senior managers to make any choices at all! The biggest strategic mistake that organizations make is not that they miss one or two choices in their decision making; it is that they do not make choices at all, something that Michael Porter alluded to a long time ago.[5]

It is amazing how many organizations fall into the trap of not making the required choices on strategy. One reason for this is the fact that these are not easy choices to make—ex ante, there are many possible answers to each one of the three questions. Should we target customer X or customer Y? Should we undertake distribution A or B? Should we offer service P or Q? Nobody knows for sure, and even though analysis could eliminate some uncertainty, it will never eliminate all of it. As a result, debates, disagreements, and politicking will precede these decisions. Yet, at the end of the day, a firm cannot be everything to everybody—it has to allocate its limited resources among the various options. Hence, clear and explicit decisions need to be made. These choices may turn out to be wrong, but that is not an excuse for not making the choices.[6]

Another reason for the failure to make the necessary choices is the fact that saying "no" to people is difficult and can often create bad feelings in the organization. If, for example, the firm decides not to target customers in Latin

America, then managers in that region will be upset because the firm will not invest resources in their region. They will oppose the decision and will be undoubtedly upset. Nobody likes to make other people upset—especially their own colleagues. Hence the desire to avoid saying "no" to people.

There may be additional reasons, but the end result is that organizations consistently and predictably fail to make the necessary choices that strategy requires. Faced with uncertainty, they invest some of their resources going after customer X and some going after customer Y—just to be on the safe side. In the process, they do a disservice to both X and Y (by underinvesting in both), but at least they ensure that they do not make a mistake by choosing one that may turn out to be wrong five or ten years down the road. Similarly, faced with the prospect of upsetting some of their colleagues, they allocate their limited resources to projects and regions that do not fit with the organization's goals or direction. In the process, they underinvest in the things that deserve their attention, but at least they do not upset their colleagues!

Failure to make choices leads to the first key reason why we have lack of clarity in strategy: Instead of being a clear statement of the (difficult) choices that the organization has made, strategy becomes nothing more than a vague and generic statement that lists all the wonderful things that the firm aims to achieve. It says all the right things so that nobody can really disagree with it, but fails to state the one thing that will offer guidance to employees—the choices the organization has made—exactly because no choices have been made. When you read the annual report of any company, what you get is good-sounding motherhood statements masquerading as strategy statements, a point also made by other academics.[7] These offer no guidance or direction to employees. No wonder these people complain that they have no idea what their organization's strategy is. They do not know it because the organization does not really have a strategy!

## Reason #2: Failure to Communicate the Choices the "Correct" Way

Assuming the firm has made explicit choices on the *who–what–how*, these choices need to be communicated to the rest of the organization. Often, this communication does not happen at all, or is so ineffective that the strategy remains a mystery to the employees. However, even in the best-case scenario when the organization has made the choices required *and* top management has spent time and energy trying to communicate these choices in a clear and explicit way, the probability is still high that employees will fail to fully understand what is communicated to them. There are two main reasons for this.

The first reason has to do with the fact that strategies are often communicated at such a general level that employees find it impossible to understand what they mean or what they can do to help implement them. For example, consider the following (real) strategy statement by an (unnamed) multinational: "Our strategy is to become a truly customer-led company and establish a platform from which to evolve and grow. We will drive innovation and value-adding integrated solutions and we will pivot to consultative customer partnerships and services business models." This statement is so generic it means nothing to people. It offers no guidance as to the direction this organization is moving in; it specifies none of the choices that have been made; and it leaves employees in the dark as to how they can help with their day-to-day actions.

Notice, also, the mixing up of goals or aspirations with how these could be achieved as well as the use of beautiful words that sound good but can mean different things to different people. For example, "value-adding integrated solutions" or "consultative customer partnerships" may mean one thing to one employee and something else to another. This, in turn, creates confusion and disagreements. To fully appreciate how serious this problem is, consider one of the most widely used phrases in business: "Think strategically." Every one of us has been advised at one point or another to "think strategically." We all agree that this is important, and we all aspire to do it. But what exactly does this phrase mean? I have asked hundreds of executives to tell me what comes to mind when somebody asks them to "think strategically." How about you? What do *you* think people mean when they tell you to think strategically? It turns out that this phrase can have many possible meanings. Among the most popular are the following:

- Think long term (at least 3–5 years into the future).
- Think about the big issues facing us (not the incremental ones).
- Start your thinking externally with the big changes and disruptions that are happening around us and then decide what to do internally.
- Do not panic; step back and think calmly about the changes around us.
- Think holistically, how the whole organization might be affected by what you want to do, not just your unit or division.
- Think about the issues collectively and cooperatively (rather than individually).
- Think about the big steps we need to be taking to achieve our vision.

These are just seven of the possible meanings of this phrase (there may be others). Now ask yourself: "What happens in an organization when the same statement can have (at least) seven possible meanings?" The obvious answer is confusion and lack of clarity. For example, your boss might have meant "think long term" when he/she asked you to think strategically, whereas you may have thought they meant "think collectively and cooperatively." You proceed to do so but then your boss gets upset that you are not doing what he/she asked you to do. This scenario happens quite frequently in organizations because senior management seems to have an insatiable appetite for buzzwords and generic statements. Phrases such as "think strategically" or "think outside the box" or "be customer-centric" or "be agile" all sound good but mean nothing to people. They are too generic to offer any guidance, and this is one key reason why the communication of our strategy often ends up confusing people rather than offering them clarity. It is also one of the reasons that led management writers Chip and Dan Heath to proclaim that "what looks like resistance to change is often lack of clarity."[8]

There is a second reason that undermines any communication campaign. Simply communicating the choices you have made is often insufficient. What you really need to do is to communicate the choice *and* the alternatives considered and rejected in favor of the choice. It is the positioning of the choice *relative* to the alternatives considered that makes the choice clear to people. This means that what you need to say is *not*: "We have decided to target customer X." Instead, you should say: "We have decided to target customer X rather than customer Y or customer Z." Furthermore, for people to appreciate that a difficult choice has indeed been made, the alternatives considered must not only be explicitly communicated to everybody, they must also be credible and viable alternatives. For example, choosing to be "the leading supplier in our markets" is not a credible choice. What alternatives to "leading supplier" have you considered and rejected? Nothing credible comes to mind and this makes this statement a non-choice.

How do you know if the alternatives you considered (and rejected) are credible and viable? A good test is to look at how many people in the organization argued in favor of the rejected alternatives. If enough people supported the rejected alternatives or argued passionately in their support, or if your eventual choice is not universally accepted, that means that the alternatives were credible ones. This is why explicitly stating what alternatives you considered (and rejected) is so important for your audience—it helps them see that you are being honest when you say you have made some difficult choices, and makes them appreciate even more the choice made.

The importance of communicating choices relative to the alternatives considered is an established concept in psychology.[9] I realized its value early in my career when as head of my department at London Business School, I undertook customer research to decide what new courses to offer to our students. Specifically, all first-year MBA students were presented with a list of possible new courses and were asked to indicate which ones they would want us to develop and offer as electives for them to take in the second year of their degree. Two courses proved to be particularly popular: a course on ethics that 86 percent of students picked and a course on sustainability that 90 percent of students picked. We spent the next few months developing the materials for these two new courses and then offered them to students as electives. Much to our surprise, fewer than 10 students (out of 400) chose to register for either of these two courses. In hindsight, the reason was obvious. The school's portfolio of elective courses listed more than 80 courses from which students had to choose 15 for their second year. The students, therefore, had to make difficult choices: Do I want to register for a course on corporate finance or a course on ethics? Both were attractive, but the course on corporate finance was obviously more attractive. Instead of asking students "Would you like us to offer you course A?," we should have been asking them: "If you had to choose between course A or course B, which one would you choose?" It was only when all the alternatives were presented that students' real preferences became evident. Similarly, it is only when all the alternatives considered are presented to people that the strategic choice we have made becomes clear.

### Reason #3: Dilution of Choices Over Time

So far, we have argued that employees do not know our strategy for two key reasons: (i) we have failed to make the necessary choices and as a result we are communicating to people good-sounding platitudes rather than a coherent strategy; and (ii) even if we have made the necessary choices, the *way* we are communicating them to people creates more confusion than clarity. There is, however, a third and perhaps more sinister reason why employees often find themselves confused when it comes to strategy.

The choices made are always decided *at a point in time*, given the market realities that the organization is facing at that point in time. Over time, these market realities might change—new competitors may emerge, different customer needs may rise in significance, new technologies may enter the industry, and so on. Given the ever-changing market realities, the organization needs to be on constant alert, changing and adapting its original choices in order to respond to the changes happening around it. Here lies one of the biggest dangers to strategy—in its efforts to respond to emerging threats or exploit new opportunities, the organization might slowly change its original choices. In the process, it might end up diluting its original choices and destroying its distinctive position in the market.

The manifestation of this will be top management saying one thing while the organization is seen doing another. For example, it may be that the strategy says that we are targeting customer X when in fact we are selling to customer X and customer Y. Consider an organization like the broker Edward Jones in the US, which built its success on a very distinctive strategy—targeting middle America and selling them financial products through an extensive one-broker office network on the promise of "peace of mind."[10] Imagine that in response to the arrival of the internet and the growth of online brokerage, it decides to offer online brokerage to its customers. The addition of this service may be seen as the most natural and obvious thing to do to exploit the rise of the internet, but in the process of doing so, Edward Jones will be diluting the distinctiveness of its strategy—it is no longer selling "peace of mind," it is selling financial products like every other firm in its industry. Over time, additional decisions like this one, taken one by one and in response to perceived threats and opportunities that emerge all the time, will lead the organization to a place far away from where it started. In other words, it will be seen doing totally different things from what its original strategy stated. Imagine being an employee in an organization whose CEO is saying one thing while you observe the organization doing another. Would you not complain that your organization does not really have a strategy—no matter what your senior management is saying?

What is the solution to this problem? Surely the organization must respond to the changes happening around it, but how can it do so without diluting its strategy? One solution is to undertake only those responses (to the external changes) that fit its chosen strategy. For example, if Edward Jones is to embrace online brokerage, it will have to implement it in ways that reinforce and support its chosen customer base and value proposition. An alternative is to accept that the responses will inevitably lead to a different strategy—accept this and more importantly, communicate the changed strategy to your employees. There is nothing wrong with changing strategy; what is wrong is to change the strategy without acknowledging this and pretending that the old strategy is still valid.

Overall, therefore, it is important that we develop a clear strategy and communicate it to our people to guide their day-to-day decisions. It has become popular to claim that strategy implementation is more important than having a strategy, or that "culture eats strategy for breakfast." Nothing could be further from the truth. Imagine that your strategy is to knock down a wall in your house by knocking your head against the wall with vigour and passion. No matter what implementation strategy you use, it is highly unlikely that you will succeed. A strategy that is built upon the choices you have made on the *who–what–how* and has been communicated to people the "proper" way is a prerequisite to everything else. Sure, you still need to implement it, and you still need to have the right culture for implementation to succeed. But just like you'll have to learn to walk before you run, a company needs to develop the correct strategy before it tries to implement it. Developing the correct strategy is not intellectually difficult—but it still requires strong leaders willing to make the difficult choices and willing to say "no."

## Parameter #2: Strong Values and a Motivating Purpose

The second parameter that can be used to guide employees' behaviors—and in the process allow us to give them a lot of autonomy—is a motivating purpose and strong, shared values. An example that highlights the importance of purpose is provided by Cathy O'Dowd, a member of the first team from South Africa that succeeded in reaching the summit of Mount Everest in 1996. The team was put together through a national competition and was given the task to symbolically place the new South African democratic flag at the top of Everest. Since the members of the team were all strangers, getting to know each other and creating a team culture were prerequisites to a successful expedition. They therefore spent a few months at base camp before attempting the climb, preparing and working together to become a team rather than a collection of individuals. This, according to O'Dowd, proved to be a challenge. It wasn't long before arguments and disagreements began to surface, and team cohesion started to erode day by day. The team split into smaller subgroups, each trying to do each other one better and competing with one another rather than collaborating. The dynamics reached such a bad state that the newspapers back home began reporting the disintegration of the team and the imminent failure of the expedition. One morning, during a particularly heated team meeting, the team leader asked the others to be quiet for a minute. He then pointed to something at the top of the tent. This was the new South African flag. He told them: "That's why we are here. Our fellow citizens have selected us to place the flag of our new country on Mount Everest and tell the world that a new South Africa has been born. Let's not let them down." This statement, according to O'Dowd, had a profound effect on the team. As if by magic, interpersonal conflict disappeared and the team members started working together to accomplish this mission. A month later, the South African flag was on top of Everest.[11]

This story highlights the importance of a motivating goal or purpose in uniting, energizing, and guiding people. Perhaps the most famous example is President Kennedy's stretch goal to put a man on the moon by the end of the 1960s—an ambition and objective that focused a nation's attention and galvanized millions of people into a collective effort. As long as people "buy into" the purpose, we can allow them a lot of autonomy to operate because we will be confident that they will only take actions that support the purpose. The same principle applies to *organizational values*. As long as employees know and believe the values of the organization, we can be confident that they will not do things that might undermine those values. When faced with a decision, they will be guided by a simple question: "Does this decision fall within the values of my organization?" If the answer is yes, they will know that they have autonomy to make this decision. If the answer is no, they will know that they cannot make the decision on their own; they need to seek guidance from their managers.

There is nothing in what we have said so far that can be considered controversial. However, there is a catch: Not all purposes are motivating and not all statements of organizational values are effective in guiding behaviors the way we have discussed here. On the contrary, if we judge by the fact that 87 percent of employees in the world claim to be disengaged or actively disengaged at work, the majority of purposes must be useless.[12] The question that we must address, therefore, is: "What is the difference between motivating and non-motivating purposes and what is the difference between values that guide behaviors versus values that are ignored by people?" Despite a widespread belief that the words used or the content of the purpose and values statements are important, the evidence suggests that they are not particularly significant factors in making these statements effective.[13] Yes, having a nice-sounding purpose (e.g. "we aim to make the world a better place") is better than having one that lacks any emotional content (e.g. "we aim to maximize shareholder value"), but the words used in the statement are not the most important factor determining its effectiveness. By far more important is whether employees have "bought into" the purpose or our statement of values. Are they truly energized by our purpose, and do they live by the values we promote, or do they consider both of them as necessary evils that they ignore at every chance? Of course, people will not "buy into" our purpose and values simply because we tell them to. We need to find ways to actively "sell" these things to employees so as to win their buy-in. This, naturally, raises the question: "How can we sell our purpose or statement of values so that our people buy into them?"

This is a topic we also raised in Chapter 3 in the context of how to sell a positive goal to people to win their emotional commitment. Even though there are similarities, the process that will help us sell the organization's purpose and values requires a few additional steps to those we discussed in Chapter 3. Specifically, an effective selling process requires that we take employees through four stages (see Figure 6.1).

In the first stage, we need to communicate our purpose and values to the employees so that at the end of the day they can all confidently say: "I know what our purpose and values are." This may sound easy to do, but it should not be underestimated because there is evidence that suggests that people always overestimate their ability to communicate clearly. For example, in an experiment undertaken by Elizabeth Newton at Stanford University, participants were asked to tap a song to a group of listeners.[14] The tappers were asked to guess what proportion of their listeners would understand what

FIGURE 6.1 How to win emotional commitment for our purpose

song they were tapping. On average, they expected 50 percent to under-stand. In reality, only 2.5 percent did. This shows that we consider ourselves better communicators than we really are. Therefore, care must be taken at this stage to make sure that our communication is clear and people really understand what we are telling them.

In the second stage, we need to explain to people the "why": Why did we pick this particular purpose and why is it important to us as an organization and to them as individuals in the organization? The same explanation should be undertaken for our choice of values. At the end of this stage, you want people to say: "I know what you want me to do and I understand why." This stage will go more smoothly if people have been involved in the develop-ment of our purpose or values.

The third stage is where we need to create belief in what we are selling to them. No matter how persuasive the two previous stages have been, your employees will probably be wondering: "Can we really achieve this purpose and do you really mean it when you say that these are the values that are important for our organization?" Creating and celebrating early victories toward the achievement of the purpose is one tactic that can make it believ-able to people. So is providing them with the necessary resources and the supporting environment to help them achieve it. Demonstrating through actions that the stated values are not only important but also take priority over financial results is probably the most effective way to create belief. If you succeed with this stage, your people will be saying: "I know what we need to do, I understand why, and I think we will do it."

The fourth stage is by far the most difficult stage in the process. This is when you go from rational acceptance to emotional commitment. The tactics described in Chapter 3—such as visualization, story-telling, and walking the talk—can also be used here to win people's hearts. Two addi-tional tactics are making your people feel special for working in your organization and making them feel they are in this together. To make people feel special, you have to make them feel unique—in other words, different from employees in other organizations. You can achieve this by treating them in different ways from everybody else, or by giving them different goals or responsibilities than they would expect in another organization, or by creating a unique and special culture around them. To make people feel that they are in this together, you have to foster a team spirit where every-body is equal and interdependent. You can also use symbols and rituals to reinforce the team spirit.

How do you know if you have succeeded in selling your purpose or values to your employees to win their buy-in? The symptoms you should look out for are people full of energy and passion, having fun while working hard, enjoying the company of their colleagues, and never missing a chance to express how proud they feel to be members of the team. For them, coming to work is a joy because it allows them to pursue something they value, with people they trust, within an organization that shares their values and beliefs. It is only when this is achieved that you should be willing to give your people as much autonomy and freedom as you can, comfortable in the thought that they will not do anything that will undermine the organization's purpose or values.

## Additional Parameters to Guide Employees

The organization's clear strategic choices and a motivating purpose along with strong values that employees have bought into are the key parameters that we need to put in place so that employees will know when to operate with autonomy and when to refer the decision to top management. Obviously, these are not the only parameters at our disposal. For example, a strong culture where people feel part of the family can also guide people's behaviors and enhance our ability to grant more autonomy. Similarly, a decentralized structure where employees belong to smaller units, each with its own leader, will also allow us to grant more autonomy because people can keep an eye on each other, and local leaders can monitor more effectively.

At the same time, we don't want to imply that these parameters can replace completely the control and monitoring systems of the organization. Of course not. Despite the best of intentions, people can still make mistakes, sometimes costly ones. We therefore need to put control systems in place to ensure that people play by the rules. In fact, our reliance on strict monitoring and control systems will increase the more bad experiences we have of people deviating from the prescribed parameters. Therefore, how much we rely on monitoring and control versus the parameters we have discussed so far will depend on the results of our efforts to grant autonomy within parameters.

## What if People "Abuse" Autonomy?

If everything goes according to plan, your people should be clear what the parameters within which they can act with autonomy are. In that case, you can expect that under most circumstances, they will behave according to plan: exercise autonomy when the decision falls within these parameters and ask for guidance and permission for any decisions that fall outside these parameters. Unfortunately, as any parent dealing with teenagers already knows, life can sometimes take unexpected turns: Teenagers may end up doing something that is clearly outside the prescribed parameters, and so do employees. This does not mean that a bad outcome will necessarily be the result. It may or it may not. The question that arises then is: Irrespective of the outcome, how should we handle the fact that an employee exercised autonomy in a situation when they should not have?

If you think this is an easy question to answer, consider the case of Stanislav Yevgrafovich Petrov. You probably never heard of this person, but he has come to be known as the man who saved the world. A documentary movie called *The Man Who Saved the World* was made in 2014 to tell his story. On 26 September 1983, just three weeks after the Soviet military had shot down Korean Air Lines Flight 007, Lieutenant General Petrov was the duty officer at the command center for the Soviet nuclear early-warning system. Much to his surprise, the system reported that a missile had been launched from the United States, followed by five additional missiles. Against Soviet military protocol, he decided that the missile attack was probably a mistake and did not proceed to launch a retaliatory nuclear attack on the US and its NATO allies, something that could have resulted in a large-scale nuclear war. As it turned out, the Soviet warning system had indeed malfunctioned and there was no missile attack from the US.

It is hard to criticize a man who saved the world from nuclear disaster, but the question that needs to be asked is: Did he act according to the principles we outlined above? The answer is unambiguously "no." For whatever reasons—plain common sense being one—he took it upon himself to make a decision that could have had disastrous consequences for his "organization." Just imagine if he had been wrong about his assessment that the Soviet early-warning system was making a mistake in reporting a US attack and that a real attack was indeed taking place. How would history have judged his decision and lack of action? There is no avoiding the fact that this man made a decision that was clearly outside any parameters we talked about. But thank God he did so, because the result was good news for the world. The question is: How should we treat this individual? Should he be punished, even fired, for doing this or should he get an award? More importantly, how can we use incidents such as this one to improve our processes and procedures?

What happened with Petrov is only one of four possible scenarios that we may face depending on whether or not employees follow the correct process outlined above and what the outcome turns out to be (see Figure 6.2). In the first scenario, employees follow the "correct" process and the outcome turns out great. This is easy: We applaud and reward these employees. In the second scenario, employees follow the correct process, but the outcome turns out to be bad. We can try to learn from the experience and improve our process, but there is no reason to blame the individuals concerned. In the third scenario, employees act outside the parameters we developed for them and the outcome is bad. Many disasters are a result of this and it is at times like these that companies put renewed emphasis on control and monitoring systems to ensure that employees do not abuse the autonomy given to them. In the fourth scenario, employees act outside the parameters we set for them, but the outcome turns out to be good—exactly what happened with Petrov. The question, once again, is: How should we treat these employees and what lessons should we draw from such incidents?

In the Soviet Union, Petrov underwent intense questioning by his superiors, was reassigned to a less sensitive post, took early retirement, and suffered a nervous breakdown. In the West, he received two World Citizen Awards, in San Francisco in 2004 and in New York in 2006, as well as the Dresden Peace Prize in Germany in 2013. He was also honored in a meeting at the United Nations in New York and was interviewed by Walter Cronkite on CBS. Obviously, there is no right answer on how to treat employees that act outside their sphere of autonomy, especially when their actions produce a desirable result. This, however, does not mean that there are no lessons to be learned or improvements to be made. Incidents such as this should be

FIGURE 6.2  Autonomy and possible outcomes

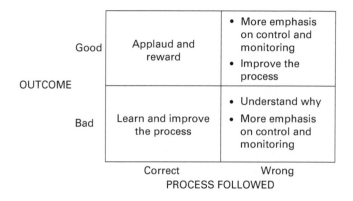

used to identify weaknesses in our processes and improve them. For example, one lesson here is that critical decisions such as launching a nuclear attack should not be the responsibility of just one individual, whatever their position in the organization. Another lesson is to ensure that proper monitoring and controls are used in the organization. There is a fine balance to be struck, but lack of monitoring in the name of autonomy is an invitation to problems. Finally, the incidents can be used to educate our people about what is appropriate for them to do and what is not. The important thing is to go beyond assigning blame and punishing individuals. If we punish the individual without improving the process, the same mistakes will be made by whoever replaces them.

## References

1  This section was originally published as: "Three reasons why your strategy could fail," *Think at London Business School*, © London Business School 2020. Reprinted with permission.

2  Tim Devinney: "When CEOs talk strategy, is anyone listening?" *Harvard Business Review*, June 2013, Vol. 91, No. 6, p. 28.

3  For example, William Schiemann found that only 14 percent of the organizations that he surveyed reported that their employees had a good understanding of their company's strategy and direction. This statistic is reported in William Schiemann: "Aligning performance management with organizational strategy, values and goals," Chapter 2, pp. 45–88 in James Smither and Manuel London: *Performance Management: Putting research into action*, San Francisco, CA: John Wiley & Sons, 2009. Another study undertaken by the consulting company Watson Wyatt reported that only 10 percent of employees and 40 percent of managers understood their organization's strategy.

4  Costas Markides: "What is strategy and how do you know if you have one?" *Business Strategy Review*, Summer 2004, Vol. 15, No. 2, pp. 5–12. A more detailed treatment can be found in Costas Markides: *All the Right Moves: A guide to crafting breakthrough strategy*, Boston, MA: HBS Press, 2000.

5  Michael Porter: "What is strategy?" *Harvard Business Review*, November–December 1996, Vol. 74, No. 6, pp. 61–78.

6  Costas Markides: *Three Reasons Why Your Strategy Could Fail*, London Business School, 2020. www.london.edu/think/three-reasons-why-your-strategy-could-fail (archived at https://perma.cc/3SKK-LUSW). This article first appeared in *Think at London Business School*. © London Business School 2020. Reprinted with permission.

**7**   Freek Vermeulen: "Many strategies fail because they are not actually strategies," *Harvard Business Review*, online edition, November 8, 2017.

**8**   Chip Heath and Dan Heath: *Switch: How to change things when change is hard*, New York: Crown Business, 2010.

**9**   Gregory Northcraft and Margaret Neale: "Opportunity costs and the framing of resource allocation decisions," *Organizational Behavior and Human Decision Processes*, 1986, Vol. 37, pp. 348–356.

**10**  Costas Markides: "Strategy as making choices: A discussion with John Bachmann, managing principal of Edward Jones," *European Management Journal*, June 1999, Vol. 17, No. 3, pp. 275–281.

**11**  Cathy O'Dowd: *Just for the Love of It*, Free to Decide Publishing, 1999.

**12**  Gallup, *State of the Global Workplace*, 2017.

**13**  Constantinos Markides and Vassilis Papadakis: "What constitutes an effective mission statement: An empirical investigation," Chapter 3, pp. 33–54 in Michael Hitt, Joan Ricart I Costa, and Robert Nixon (eds.): *New Managerial Mindsets: Organizational transformation and strategy implementation*, Chichester, UK: John Wiley & Sons Ltd, 1998.

**14**  Chip Heath and Dan Heath: "The curse of knowledge," *Harvard Business Review*, December 2006, pp. 20–22.

•

# 07

# Exploit the Disruption

*The Importance of an Innovative Strategy of Response*

So far, we have explored how you can put in place the right foundations for the organization to spring into action as soon as a disruption appears on the horizon—such as the correct attitude toward disruption, a positive sense of urgency throughout the organization, and an underlying organizational environment that supports and promotes the behaviors of agility. Unfortunately, all this preparation will be for nothing unless we also put in place the right conditions—such as the right processes and the right people—to ensure that we develop a good strategy of response. We will explore how to do this in this chapter and the next, but it is important to stress at the very beginning that our goal is to discuss *the thinking process* that will ensure you develop a good strategy rather than explore what specific strategy you should adopt.

Different organizations face different disruptions, so it is impossible for anybody to tell you what strategy to adopt without knowing the specific disruption you need to respond to. In this sense, the question "What strategy should I adopt to respond to disruption?" makes no sense. The word "disruption" is a generic term that lacks clarity. Asking the generic question "How should I respond to disruption?" is analogous to asking your doctor "How should I respond to disease?" You would (and should) be worried if your doctor prescribed a medicine to you without first determining your disease.

## The Ingredients of Successful Response

We cannot prescribe the strategy that every firm should follow, but we can explore how to approach the task. How, then, should an organization go about developing an effective strategy of response? It may help to explain what an effective strategy of response looks like before exploring how to develop it. We will consider three examples—one of successful response and the other two of failed responses.

### A Successful Response: TAG Heuer Versus the Apple Watch[1]

On September 9, 2014, during a press event at which the iPhone 6 was also presented, Apple CEO Tim Cook announced the introduction of the Apple smartwatch. The announcement was not a surprise—rumors that Apple was developing a wearable device had been circulating since 2011. But the actual announcement sent shockwaves through the global watch industry. At the time of Apple's announcement, analysts were confident of the smartwatch's market potential. A Citi analyst estimated: "The market could be worth $10 billion by 2018."[2] Cook focused on Apple's desire to "make the best watch in the world,"[3] in terms not only of accuracy but also of customization. The watch was also being positioned as a fashion item. Elmar Mock, one of the inventors of the Swatch watch, predicted that smartwatches could affect up to 30 percent of the traditional watch industry: "In the short term it is not danger knocking on the door but opportunity, and it would be a shame if the Swiss watchmakers didn't take it."[4] The Apple watch was released on April 24, 2015 and quickly became the best-selling wearable device, with 4.2 million sold in the second quarter of 2015 alone. Its first announced price was "starting at $349."

One of the established competitors that felt threatened by the Apple watch was LVMH, the French luxury goods conglomerate. The watch division of LVMH owned three brands—Hublot at the high end of the market, Zenith in mid-range, and TAG Heuer at the low end. The division was run by an industry veteran, Jean-Claude Biver, who felt that the Apple watch was particularly disruptive for his low-end brand, TAG Heuer. Biver did not want to simply sit and wait to see what Apple produced and then respond; he wanted to be proactive and develop a response even before Apple introduced its new product. He described his position as follows: "I consider myself to be in the watch industry. There is no question that the smartwatch will fundamentally change our industry, so I need to respond to it."

Having decided that TAG Heuer was the brand that needed to respond, Biver took the key decision early on to develop a watch that was as differentiated from the Apple version as possible. Talking to a reporter in 2014, Biver argued that "a simple variation of the Apple watch did not interest him." He wanted his smartwatch to be different and unique.[5] He considered two options. The first was to create an entirely new brand. The second was to use the TAG Heuer brand and create a smartwatch as a new model with the TAG branding and personality. He decided on the latter. Rather than call it a smartwatch, he called the line the "Connected Watch." This gave birth to the TAG Heuer Connected, which was officially announced in March 2015, one month *before* the Apple watch was released.

Among the many challenges that Biver faced in introducing the TAG Heuer Connected watch, three stood out:

- How to produce or source the technology and the parts for a Connected watch keeping in mind the small volume of units that he planned to sell.
- How to safeguard the DNA of the TAG Heuer brand—which was "eternity"—on a watch whose technology changed every few years.
- At what price to introduce the new watch.

The first challenge Biver faced was that nobody in Switzerland or LVMH could actually produce a smartwatch: "We will never be capable in Switzerland of producing all the parts of the Connected watch. We can produce 70–80 percent but we can't produce the most important part, the microprocessors, because it is extremely costly and extremely sophisticated. There are only a handful of companies in the world producing these types of microprocessors." Touchscreen technology was another issue. The Chinese were the best manufacturers of touchscreens, but they were used to delivering high volumes—a minimum of 1 million units per order. At best, TAG Heuer needed an order of just 10,000–20,000 units for a launch. When Biver's team approached the Chinese manufacturers, they refused any order less than the minimum quantity. No manufacturer would sell such a low volume at a reasonable price including the cost of tooling and casting for production, which had to be built into the price. Where would the touchscreens come from then? It was a similar story with the batteries. TAG Heuer was not used to playing in the mass market. The Chinese were not used to supplying such small quantities.

Production aside, there were serious risks to the brand that couldn't be dismissed. TAG Heuer had its own distinctive look and its own DNA that made it instantly recognisable. The challenge for Biver was to create a smartwatch that on the one hand was a Connected watch but at the same time a TAG Heuer watch. As he put it: "I must keep my DNA whatever happens—when people see my Connected smartwatch, they should not detect that it is a Connected watch. They must see that it is a TAG Heuer. If they don't see the DNA of a TAG Heuer in the Connected watch, then I have failed." That meant that the design had to be distinctively TAG Heuer. This was a challenge in itself because most smartwatches were small and thin, compared with the aggressive and large TAG watches.

TAG's traditional selling proposition was the concept of "eternity." Unlike all the smartwatches on the market, TAG Heuer could not make a "throwaway watch," something that in 2–5 years would be discarded. The risk to the brand was too high. As Biver put it: "This is not good for the reputation of the brand because we sell watches that cost four to eight thousand dollars. At that price, customers would never think they bought something that can be thrown away after a few years. We cannot have this bad reputation as it would be too easy for the competition to play on that and to promote that side against us." The problem he was facing was that the technology of the Connected watch would change every few years. How, then, can you create something that may need to be changed every few years and still sell it on the concept of "eternity"?

Another challenge was pricing. A normal TAG Heuer was retailing at about $2,600. Biver had decided upon this price when he made the decision that the TAG Heuer should be positioned away from the price point of Zenith (to avoid internal competition) and close to the "affordable luxury" entry point for consumers. The Apple watch, by contrast, was retailing for $349–399. There was a reason for that. The relatively short lifespan of the technology in a smartwatch meant that customers would need to replace it every one or two years, as technology improved. How much can you charge for a product that the consumer will throw away in a couple of years? LVMH and TAG Heuer made watches that would last for eternity. They weren't "thrown away" in the same way that a smartphone or smartwatches were.

One by one, Biver set about to overcome the challenges facing him, with the aim of announcing a new smartwatch before the introduction of the Apple watch. He first solved his production problems by entering into an alliance with Intel and Google to produce the TAG Heuer Connected watch. Google was tasked with developing the software for the watch, as it was to be Android based. Intel was asked to provide the microprocessor. Intel helped in another area as well, convincing a Chinese touchscreen company to deliver 150,000 touchscreens to TAG. While this was considerably more than the 10,000 TAG initially wanted, it was a lot less than the 1 million minimum that Chinese manufacturers insisted upon. How did Biver convince two of the biggest technology companies in the world to partner with him for such a small venture? His selling proposition was that by partnering with him, they could learn about the world of luxury, something that might help them in upgrading their own products. His view was that among the big technology firms, only Apple had succeeded in achieving luxury status. Other technology firms, such as Intel and Google, might partner with TAG Heuer to learn about the luxury market.

To overcome the obsolescence issue and create a watch that had a life beyond the life of the technology, Biver came up with the solution of the "modular watch." Essentially this meant that the watch was sold as a case into which different "modules" could be inserted. The first Connected watch had two modules—the traditional TAG Heuer mechanical module and the electronic Connected module. Consumers could easily and quickly remove one module and insert the other, depending on their mood. As Biver said: "If you wake up in the morning and you feel young and tech-savvy, you insert the electronic module in your watch. In the evening, when you go to the opera and want to feel a little bit more serious, you remove the electronic module and insert the mechanical module in your watch." The plan was to develop more modules in the future. Customers could buy the Connected watch on its own (with only the smartwatch module) or with the option of additional modules.

To develop the modular watch, engineers at TAG designed special lugs which held the module in the case. This was rather like a Leica camera where the owner could change the lens but the body of the camera remained the same, giving it an extended life for the high initial price. The module itself would look exactly like a TAG Heuer mechanical watch face, except that the Connected module would be a screen rather than a mechanical watch.

Each module had its own price. The smartwatch module started at $1,500. For an additional $1,500, customers could purchase a special edition Carrera mechanical module to replace the smartwatch module. This mechanical module was only available for TAG Heuer Connected watch owners. This module would then turn the watch into a classic TAG Heuer with an "eternal" long life, as though they had bought an original TAG Heuer classic watch. In addition, follow-up options were being designed so that in the future customers could purchase four different modules—a Connected module, a mechanical module, a chronograph module, and a tourbillon module. The tourbillon was the most expensive at $15,000. A lady's Connected watch was expected to be unveiled as well.

The Connected watch was compatible with both Android and Apple iOS, although the watch ran better on Android, as apps from Google Play could not be downloaded to an iPhone. The Connected watch provided notifications and health checks, much the same as many smartwatches, and three custom timekeeping applications were built into the module. What made the Connected watch unique and different from other smartwatches on the market was that it looked exactly like a TAG Heuer—the distinct look and feel and use of metals that TAG Heuer prided itself on. As one reviewer described it: "The TAG Heuer Connected watch has striking, aggressive looks, it's made from luxury materials…it is the most fashionable way of adding smart functions to your wrist."[6]

At the New York launch in November 2015, TAG Heuer received 1 billion hits on social media and had 900 million people watching the 200 TV stations that reported the launch. This was priceless PR that confirmed to Biver the correctness of his decision to launch the Connected watch with TAG Heuer rather than to create a new brand. The early success of the launch did not fool Biver, however. He knew that the Connected watch was facing serious challenges going forward. One such challenge was the evolution of the watch into a phone. According to Biver: "I'm not in technology and I cannot foresee all the improvements that will be made. What I can foresee is the day when the watch will do all the phone functions, including being a phone. When that happens, TAG Heuer might have a problem because we will need telecoms providers. Apple is in this business already, we are not. For us it's the biggest challenge. Right now, we sell our watches through retailers. If you buy a Connected watch with phone functions, you cannot use it if you buy it in one of these stores, you need to go to a phone provider. For us, it means we are losing our traditional distribution network. We cannot even sell online because for every country, we will need a contract with a provider in that country." Initial efforts to form an alliance with AT&T in the US did not bear fruit.

Another challenge was how to maintain interest in the product once the novelty had worn off. One idea was to develop apps specifically for the watch. Biver believed the direction could be sport and health, with sensors built into the watch that, due to its proximity to the body, could measure different things that a phone could not. His problem was that TAG Heuer did not have sufficient R&D muscle and would have to invest heavily. Hence the need to find a possible partner arose—perhaps a telecoms provider or a car brand.

Despite these challenges and the watch's uncertain future, Biver had no doubts that his response to the Apple watch was a success. In his own words: "It's a revolution. It will change the face of watchmaking. Apple, Samsung, LG—they cannot follow us because they don't have the mechanical movements. That's our way to escape the competition. The customer can make their watch individual. And they take no risk. The watch never becomes obsolete."[7]

Biver's claim that his new watch is a revolution might be an exaggeration, but there is no question that the TAG Heuer Connected watch has been successful so far. The team responsible for it grew from 4 members to 30 in five years, and new watch models introduced every year continued to emphasize craftsmanship and premium looks while incorporating cutting-edge sports features and apps. In March 2020, an industry analyst reported that the TAG Heuer Connected watch was "one of the only genuine alternatives to Apple remaining [in the market]...TAG Heuer's approach to add sports features while refining the watch-like smartwatch experience makes a lot of sense."[8]

## A Failed Response: Continental Airlines Versus Southwest

Like all established airline companies, Continental Airlines had to decide how to respond to the growth of the low-cost, no-frills, point-to-point business model in the airline industry. This business model emerged in the US in the 1970s (with Southwest being the pioneer) and spread to Europe and the rest of the world during the 1980s and 1990s. In contrast to the traditional airlines, low-cost players provided minimal yet good enough service and network coverage with superior price and punctuality. The model is based on direct routes, frequent departures, quick turnaround times, punctuality, no frills on board, no seat class distinctions, and cheap prices. The model is best suited to short flights of not more than around 2.5 hours and is typically used by tourists but also businesspeople on short-haul flights.

The new business model had created a huge new market partly by stealing price-sensitive customers from the established companies but primarily by attracting into the market people who normally wouldn't have traveled had it not been for the cheap and convenient flights (or would have used a different mode of transportation such as trains). To the established players, the low-end market looked like low-hanging fruit, ready for the picking. After all, flying is flying. Sure, the new business model was different from the full-service, hub-and-spoke business model that the established companies used, but nobody knew the airline market as well as they did. It was therefore frustrating for them to see competitor after competitor trying their luck with this new business model and not having much success—prominent examples being KLM and BA.

Continental, one of the top five airlines in North America before deregulation, thought it could do better than the other established airline companies. Its main customer base was business travelers, but the huge growth of the low-end market presented it with an opportunity to grow and get out of its (second) Chapter 11 bankruptcy in 1993. Under the leadership of CEO Robert Ferguson, Continental created a separate unit in 1993, called it Continental Lite, and set out to replicate the Southwest strategy on the East Coast, before Southwest could become established there.

Even though Continental Lite was set up as a separate business unit, it began life with planes taken from Continental's unprofitable Denver hub. Like Southwest, its goal was to compete on price and it tried to make this a profitable objective by mimicking many of Southwest's activities. It eliminated first-class service and on-board meals, shortened turnaround times at the gates, and increased departure frequency. However, even before the flights started, there was commentary in the press that the pilots, who would come across with the planes from the Denver hub, would not take a salary cut to make the new airline competitive with its low-cost rivals. In addition, Continental Lite continued to offer seat assignments, awarded frequent-flier awards, provided baggage checking, and refused to abandon the use of travel agents—something that would have damaged the travel agents' relationship with its parent.

Additional compromises were made. Because customers were irked by the fact that they were not able to get the same benefits on the much lower Lite fares, Continental reduced the awards on its entire frequent-flier program. Similarly, Continental could not afford to pay standard travel agent commissions on Lite fares but could not run its full-service business without the support of the travel agents—it therefore decided to resolve this dilemma by cutting commissions across the board.

Despite these weaknesses, the new airline got off to a good start and demand for its services was strong. In press releases at the time, Continental expressed the wish that Continental Lite would grow to become a third of its business. It also suggested that the only constraint preventing the no-frills airline from growing faster was the shortage of planes. In order to support its growth, Continental continued to transfer planes from the existing business to the new one.

However, soon afterwards, problems began to emerge across the whole company. The most serious was the declining quality of service for passengers on both airlines. For example, congestion and baggage transfers at Continental's hub cities caused numerous late flights and cancellations. The company quickly gained the reputation for having the worst service in the industry. After only one year of operations, one commentator remarked: "Continental Lite lost tons of money its first year and did everything possible to disappoint passengers. Continental manages month after month to be the airline that loses the most baggage and the worst or near worst in arriving on time. It is also the airline that passengers complain about the most to the U.S. Department of Transportation. I believe this triple crown of incompetence is the reason for Continental Lite's troubles. Cheap isn't enough if the service stinks."[9]

By 1994, Continental Lite had grown to become half of Continental's total operations. It had around 100 planes and was operating nearly 1,000 flights per week. However, its reputation was going from bad to worse. More worrisome, the constant negative publicity began to damage the reputation of the parent company, with passengers confusing Continental Lite with Continental and complaining that even the parent company had dropped its standards to unacceptable levels. Slowly but surely, they started leaving both airlines in large numbers.

Despite having one of the lowest operating costs per air mile in the North American airline industry, Continental Lite could not turn a profit. On the contrary, the operation was a money-losing black hole. Ferguson resigned as CEO in October 1994 and his replacement, Gordon Bethune, decided to shut down Continental Lite. The whole adventure cannot be considered anything but a failure. Continental itself merged with United Airlines in March 2012 and ceased to exist as an independent company.

### Another Failed Response: Edipresse Group Versus Free Daily Newspapers[10]

From the mid-1990s, newspaper companies around the world had to confront a series of disruptions in their markets. Perhaps the most serious was the arrival of online distribution of news and the devastating effect the internet had on print newspapers. Another equally disturbing disruption was the growth of the "free" newspaper business model. In early 2005, the

Swiss-based media company Edipresse decided to defend itself against the intrusion of this business model in its home market, the French-speaking part of Switzerland.

The first free newspaper in Switzerland, *20 Minuten*, was launched in Zurich in 1999 by a Norwegian media conglomerate. It was a big success, quickly growing to a daily circulation that was second only to *Blick*, the paid daily tabloid. Within a year, it expanded into other Swiss-German regions such as Berne, Basel, and St. Gallen so that it could benefit from printing, distribution, and overhead economies of scale while offering a larger coverage area to advertisers. In 2005, it was sold to Tamedia, Switzerland's largest media company. By then, *20 Minuten* had become the most widely read daily in Switzerland with an audited distribution of 329,000 copies and a readership of 782,000. Tamedia immediately let it be known that it planned to expand the paper in the second half of the year into the French part of Switzerland—the area Edipresse considered its own territory.

It was in this context that Edipresse announced the launch of its own free daily newspaper *Le Matin Bleu* in October 2005. Even though Edipresse operated in the French-speaking part of the country, it knew it was only a matter of time before *20 Minuten* attacked its home turf. To pre-empt its imminent arrival, *Le Matin Bleu* was launched with two editions—one in Geneva and one in Lausanne. The new daily tabloid targeted the young, urban working population in the Lake Geneva region. It complemented the group's paying newspaper *Le Matin*, which was already the most-read newspaper in French-speaking Switzerland with 353,000 readers. Theo Bouchat, the project leader and head of one of Edipresse's newspaper divisions, saw the new free daily as a concise yet complete newspaper that would offer the best advertising platform in French-speaking Switzerland. He appointed an Edipresse employee from one of its paid daily newspapers to serve as chief editor of the new free daily, but the majority of *Le Matin Bleu*'s staff—outside of the technical, printing, and distribution staff—were new to the company, young, and relatively inexperienced. Since the paper would be distributed to readers free of charge, it was critical to keep costs, including salaries, low.

Nevertheless, Bouchat was determined to give the staff of *Le Matin Bleu* every opportunity to make a success of the free paper. According to Bouchat: "We said, 'no concessions.' We didn't take anything off the table to protect our paid daily newspaper. We told them they were free to do whatever needed to be done—regardless of the effect it would have on *Le Matin*." As a result, *Le Matin Bleu* set advertising rates that were competitive with those of other free newspapers but far lower than *Le Matin*'s rates. The newspaper was similar in design and format to the paid daily but was significantly different editorially. Although both papers were tabloids, the paid newspaper was filled with in-depth news stories and editorials and was aimed at older, more traditional newspaper readers. *Le Matin Bleu* catered to younger commuters, with breezy stories and trend/style features, and no editorial commentary.

In February 2006, Tamedia announced plans to enter the market with Lausanne and Geneva regional editions of *20 Minuten* planned for March 2006. In response, *Le Matin Bleu* grew circulation quickly and by the time of the *20 Minuten* launch, it was distributing 150,000 copies per day, eclipsing *20 Minuten*'s 100,000 copies. *Le Matin Bleu* also had a first-mover advantage for selling advertising. "We already had a base of advertisers, and *20 Minuten* had no alliances when they came in," noted Bouchat. Edipresse offered an advertising package called "Top Deal," which bundled advertising in both of its newspapers. Competition for advertisers was fierce, however, and *20 Minuten* proved to have an advantage of its own: national coverage. "They were able to offer advertisers reach into the French part of Switzerland for very little additional cost," said Bouchat.

Although *Le Matin Bleu* had raised its advertising rates by 30 percent in September 2007, by early 2008 both free dailies offered similar advertising rates and were experiencing significant pressure from advertisers to keep rates down. Bouchat found that the advertisers drawn to *Le Matin Bleu* were smaller and more price-sensitive than those who advertised in *Le Matin*. "We found that most of our new clients were local businesses that could not afford to advertise in a paid daily before," he said. "*Le Matin Bleu* gave us an opportunity to re-contact advertisers who could not afford *Le Matin* or who wanted a younger demographic."

Shortly after *20 Minuten*'s arrival, Edipresse noted a troubling trend: its paid daily was beginning to lose readers. By March 2008, it had lost 20,000 readers—15 percent of its circulation—as well as some of its advertisers. "We found that the advertising cake did not become bigger," said Bouchat. "Instead, advertisers spread their ads around to two, new, cheaper newspapers." In the meantime, circulation for the free dailies continued to grow; indeed, there were more free daily papers in the market every day than paid circulation newspapers.

Bouchat felt that Edipresse had proven its ability to successfully launch a free daily. But while he believed the market could sustain one free paper, he was less optimistic about the long-term market for two free dailies. "We are far from breakeven. We had hoped for breakeven in three to four years but we are now in our third year and it is nowhere in sight," said Bouchat. The situation was made even worse by the rise of online distribution of news. While Edipresse was fighting a battle with free dailies, customers were migrating toward digital news at an alarming rate. In March 2009, Tamedia announced the acquisition of Edipresse. As part of the deal, *Le Matin Bleu* and *20 Minuten* were to be merged.

## The Key Difference: Attack, Don't Just Defend

There are obviously many things that determine whether a strategy will be successful or not. A key one that these examples highlight is that an effective strategy of response must avoid imitating what others have done in response to the disruption and should instead help the firm differentiate itself as much as possible. Simply trying to be better than the disruptors themselves or the other industry rivals responding to the same disruption is not enough. In this sense, the firm is not looking for a strategy of response—it is looking for a strategy that will allow it to reposition and differentiate itself by taking advantage of the disruption. For example, TAG Heuer did not simply try to match the Apple watch or even be better than it. Instead, it exploited the disruption to create something new that shifted the basis of competition away from the traditional strengths of the disruptor, Apple. Swatch did something similar 40 years ago in facing up to the disruption of cheap, electronic watches like Seiko and Timex. By contrast, Continental Lite tried to compete head on with the disruptor, Southwest Airlines. It basically adopted the same strategy as Southwest and tried to win by being better. This almost never works.

It all sounds easy and straightforward, but for every example of an organization that adopted an innovative response to disruption, we can name one that did not. Consider, for example, Microsoft. In 2020, everybody seemed impressed by the radical transformation that Microsoft underwent under Satya Nadella, but the same company spent the better part of the first two decades of this century going from one disaster to another by failing to respond creatively to disruption after disruption. The following quote from a May 2009 *Forbes* article by Victoria Barret captures the essence of this argument well: "Microsoft has spent hundreds of millions (and likely close to billions) trying to out do Google at search. Now the folks in Redmond have something new up their pale blue Oxfords. Microsoft is debuting a search engine, code-named 'Kumo.' If it's anything like Google, no one will care. There are lots of good-enough search alternatives out there. To unseat Google, Microsoft has to be sly. Building a 'robust search experience, Microsoft will have to shock and awe...[11]

As another example, consider the challenge of responding to a new disruptive business model that an increasing number of companies are now facing. Although there are many possible responses,[12] one of the most challenging is how to adopt the new business model next to the core business model. The most frequent advice given to established companies is to place the second business model in a separate unit and allow it to have its own name, culture, and strategy. This is the "innovator's solution" primarily associated with Clay Christensen's work on disruptive innovation, but other academics have advocated it as well.[13] Although this solution is theoretically appealing, there is now enough evidence to show that many established companies that have adopted the proposed solution have not fared very well—see, for example, the unfortunate fate of the separate units that companies like British Airways, KLM, Continental, and United developed in the airline industry.

Why is that? Because over and above creating a separate unit, the company needs to make sure that the separate unit adopts an innovative strategy—one that does not imitate the disruptor but instead attacks the market created by disruption like a guerrilla. Failure to adopt an innovative strategy will most probably doom the response. For example, in May 2020, the Royal Bank of Scotland announced that it was shutting down its separate unit (called Bo), which was supposed to exploit digital banking and rival fintechs such as Monzo and Revolut. According to one analyst: "Bo was always going to have a tough time attracting customers given the crowded nature and maturity of the digital banking market in the U.K.

It needed to find a way to stand out and establish a USP (unique selling point) to differentiate itself from the digital-only banks."[14] Unfortunately, it failed to do so, hence the closing of the brand. The bank's CEO said the bank managed to attract just 11,000 customers. This included "friends and family" of the bank — in the almost six months since it launched. That was a far cry from Revolut's more than 10 million users and Monzo's 3.5 million signups.[15]

All this suggests that while the idea is simple enough—just develop an innovative strategy of response—the reality is that established firms face formidable obstacles in following such advice. First, there is the issue of actually coming up with an innovative strategy, capable of exploiting the disruption rather than simply defending against it, a topic we tackle in the next chapter. Even when the firm succeeds in designing an innovative strategy, serious problems with implementation inevitably surface. Prominent among them is the fact that as the firm makes the transition to a new way of operating, the legacy business will suffer. This was a problem that the German newspaper group Axel Springer faced as it exploited disruption to move into a number of platform businesses, and was a problem for Microsoft as it moved away from its Windows business toward cloud computing. How do you make the transition when all the resources and power reside with the legacy business? This is a topic we will tackle later in the book. First, let's explore how a company can develop a truly *innovative* strategy of response.

## References

1   This account is based on the case study by Daniel Oyon, Costas Markides, and L. Duke: "The battle for the wrist: Tag Heuer and the Connected watch," London Business School, 2016. Reprinted with permission.

2   James Shotter and Tim Bradshaw: "Apple Watch starts countdown on face off with Swiss industry," *Financial Times*, 2014. www.ft.com/content/2421ccd0-5dca-11e4-897f-00144feabdc0 (archived at https://perma.cc/VBW3-3F5P).

3   Dan Howarth: "'We set out to create the best watch in the world' says Apple's Tim Cook," *Deezen.com*, 2014. www.dezeen.com/2014/09/09/apple-watch-unveiled/ (archived at https://perma.cc/2R8W-LU96).

4   James Shotter and Tim Bradshaw: "Apple Watch starts countdown on face off with Swiss industry," *Financial Times,* 2014. www.ft.com/content/2421ccd0-5dca-11e4-897f-00144feabdc0 (archived at https://perma.cc/H2EB-EM32).

5   S. Peca: "Jean-Claude Biver: 'Il y a forcément des dissidents' chez Tag Heuer," *Le Temps*, December 17, 2014.

6   Andrew Hoyle: "TAG Heuer Connected Watch review: The most fashionable Android Wear watch comes at a price," CNET, 2016. www.cnet.com/products/tag-heuer-connected-watch/ (archived at https://perma.cc/8QMR-TEYB).

7   Robin Swithinbank: "TAG Heuer's revolution: It's a smartwatch. It's a mechanical watch, too," *The New York Times*, 2017. www.nytimes.com/2017/03/23/fashion/watches-smartwatches-tag-heuer.html?_r=1 (archived at https://perma.cc/VJX3-HX2R).

8   Sophie Charara: "The Apple Watch won but TAG Heuer is keeping a certain kind of smartwatch alive," *Wired*, March 12, 2020.

9   Clark Howard: "Travellers Aid tips and resources to help you along budget traveller," *The Atlanta Journal – Constitution*, January 1, 1995.

10  This account is based on the case study by Daniel Oyon, Costas Markides, and Laura Winig: "Edipresse: Responding to a strategic innovation," London Business School, 2008. Reprinted with permission.

11  Victoria Barret: "Disrupting the disruptor," *Forbes.com*, May 20, 2009.

12  Constantinos Charitou and Costas Markides: "Responses to disruptive strategic innovation," *Sloan Management Review*, Winter 2003, Vol. 44, No. 2, pp. 55–63.

13  Clayton Christensen: *The Innovator's Dilemma: When new technologies cause great firms to fail*, Boston, MA: Harvard Business School Press, 1997; Clark Gilbert and Joseph Bower: "Disruptive change: When trying harder is part of the problem," *Harvard Business Review*, May 2002, pp. 3–8.

14  Ryan Browne: "One of Britain's largest banks tried to rival fintechs like Monzo and Revolut—here's why it has failed," *CNBC.com*, May 1, 2020.

15  Ibid.

# 08

# How to Develop an Innovative Strategy of Response

The failure of Kodak to successfully make the transition to digital photography, a technology it invented, is probably one of the most frequently told stories of corporate failure. Many possible reasons have been proposed for this and there is no doubt that such a spectacular failure can only be the result of numerous factors, not just one or two.[1] However, two actions by Kodak give us a glimpse of one of the most important of these factors. The first was Kodak's decision to acquire Ofoto, a file-sharing site, and then use it to get people to print digital images rather than share them online. The second was its investment in developing the Advantix Preview film and camera system, a digital camera that still required users to use film and print their photos if they wanted to keep copies. Both decisions give us a hint as to how Kodak viewed and approached the disruption in its industry: as a means to improve and grow its core business of film and printing.

A very similar story can be told about the demise of Blockbuster in the video-rental business.[2] Although it is true that the company was guilty of a late reaction to the threat posed by Netflix, nobody can deny that it eventually responded by launching Blockbuster Online as well as the service Total Access, which allowed customers to rent videos online and return them either by mail or in stores. As an added bonus, customers who returned the video to the store would receive a free in-store rental. Both actions aimed to improve the core business by combining movies-by-mail with the flexibility to pop into a local store and have personal service if needed. The strategy was favorably received at the time, yet, like the Kodak strategy, it failed to protect Blockbuster from bankruptcy.

Both Kodak and Blockbuster tried to leverage the disruptions in their respective industries to improve their core business. What is wrong with that? We can name scores of companies doing exactly the same thing, and unlike Kodak or Blockbuster, they all seem to be doing well. For example, retailers such as Walmart in the US and Waitrose in the UK are using digital technologies along with big data and robotics to improve their core business.[3] The same is true for banks such as J.P. Morgan in the US and KBC Bank in Belgium, newspaper companies such as *The New York Times* and *The Guardian*, FMCG companies such as Nestlé and Unilever, pharma companies such as Novartis and Roche, and car manufacturers such as Daimler and Toyota.[4] In industry after industry, we see companies exploiting the new disruptive technologies of the social era to improve their core businesses. Therefore, it is hard to blame Kodak or Blockbuster for doing the same. So, why did this strategy backfire on them?

The answer is deceptively simple. *Before* deciding how to use the disruptive technologies to improve the core business, an assessment needs to be made as to whether the core business is worth saving or improving in the first place. For example, before doing anything, Kodak should have asked: "Given the new realities, is the printing of photos a viable business for us to fight for?" Similarly, Blockbuster should have asked: "Is the physical distribution of movies a viable business for the future?" If your core business is marching toward oblivion, there is no sense in trying to improve it.

## Think Like an Entrepreneur

The interesting question, of course, is why didn't Kodak or Blockbuster ask these questions? If it's so obvious to us now, how come they missed it? One answer may be that they did ask the questions but for whatever reason made the assessment that their core businesses were worth fighting for. How likely is this scenario? Well, if you approach the question in a "biased" way, chances are you will get a biased answer. Another way of saying this is that if you approach the question with the eyes of a manager from the core business, you are likely to see the future unfolding in a more favorable way for the core business than someone who approaches the question with fresh eyes. Plus, you are likely to be more emotionally invested in ensuring the success of the core business than somebody who never spent a minute inside the business.

All this carries a huge implication for leaders who need to develop a response strategy: They need to approach disruption with eyes that are free of the biases of the core business. In other words, they need to step outside the mindset of the core business and think from different perspectives—for example, think like an entrepreneur, or like a new entrant, or from the perspective of a stakeholder they really care about, such as customers or a regulator or shareholders. My favorite is to approach the task like an entrepreneur. By this I mean that during the thinking process, we need to forget the core business altogether and ask ourselves: "If I was an entrepreneur entering the markets created by disruption, what strategy would I have adopted?" The idea is to look at the new market without the constraints of the core business and come up with a strategy whose aim is to make you a winner in the *new* market as opposed to making you a winner in your *core* market.

Imagine if Kodak had taken this first step in its strategic analysis. Instead of asking itself "How can I use the new technologies to improve my core business?" it should have asked: "If I was an entrepreneur like Richard Branson, thinking about entering the market of digital photography, what strategy would I adopt?" Had Kodak asked this question, it would never have come up with the idea of a digital camera that still required consumers to print their photos! Such an idea can only emerge from the minds of managers who are preoccupied with the survival of the core business and can only think of ways to exploit the disruption in order to save or improve the core business. An entrepreneur would never think like this, simply because they do not have a core business to worry about.

This is the cardinal mistake that many established companies make in trying to develop a response strategy. They start their thinking with their core business in mind and extrapolate to what they need to do to exploit the disruption for the sake of the core business. As a result, the needs and requirements of the core business cloud and constrain their thinking. Instead, they should start thinking like an entrepreneur, free of the constraints of the core business. The result will be a strategy that *may* build upon the existing business or may just disregard the core business entirely. This does not mean that we forget about the core business completely. *After* a strategy is formulated, we can then start thinking how to utilize the assets and knowledge that reside within the core business to help us implement the new strategy more quickly and more efficiently than an entrepreneur. But the important thing is to *first* develop the strategy without worrying about the core business and then utilize the competencies of the core business to implement the strategy developed.

All this suggests that *how* we approach the task of developing an effective strategy of response is as important as *what* strategy we adopt. Whatever business they are in, companies must start their thinking like an entrepreneur. In other words, they must start with the new realities created by the disruption, identify what they need to do to be successful given the new realities, and then decide whether the existing core business will be part of the new strategy or whether they should take a totally different path, away from the core business. Only after they have decided on the path they will take should the core business be brought back into the analysis, with the question: "How can we utilize the assets, competencies, and knowledge of the core business to help in the implementation of the new path we have chosen?"

## A Framework to Think About Response

Starting our thinking with a clean slate is a good start. But we still need to come up with a strategy of response. The point to appreciate at this stage is that there is no single strategy that is optimal for all. First, there is the issue that different companies may be facing different disruptions. Each company must therefore develop a strategy for the specific disruption that is affecting its business. More importantly, even for companies facing the same disruption, the appropriate response will depend on their firm-specific circumstances. What is appropriate for one company may not be so for another company. For example, consider how banks have responded to digital banking. It may be the same disruption for all, yet banks have responded to it in different ways. Most of them chose to incorporate this way of doing business into their existing business model, whereas banks such as BNP Paribas and Royal Bank of Scotland have chosen to set up separate units to develop the digital banking market. The point is that there is no single response that is optimal for all firms. Many factors will influence which response is the best one for a given firm, including aspects such as the company's position in the industry, its competencies, the rate at which the disruption is growing, the nature of the innovator that introduced the disruption, and how aggressively the firm wants to pursue the market created by disruption.

FIGURE 8.1  Developing a strategy of response

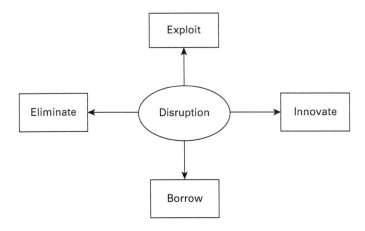

In developing a response strategy, it is best to approach the task in a struc-tured way. The framework presented in Figure 8.1 is one such approach. Obviously, the four issues that this framework presents are not the only ones to consider, but going through these four will bring to the surface most of the critical issues that need to be addressed. Let's explore in more detail the four questions that this framework raises.

### Exploit Disruptors' Weaknesses

Every disruption gives rise to new realities that will, in turn, allow some companies—usually newcomers to the industry—to thrive. These are companies that develop new business models to leverage the new technolo-gies and exploit the opportunities that the disruption has created. They may look formidable and unbeatable, especially at the start of the disruption when most incumbents are caught off guard, but the truth is that they are not perfect. Any business model, no matter how good, has weaknesses in it. The first question to explore, therefore, is: "What are the weaknesses in the disruptors' strategies and how can I develop a strategy to exploit them?" Remember, you have an advantage over the disruptors. You have assets, competencies, and knowledge from the core business that you can now leverage to develop a strategy that undermines the disruptors' strategy by exploiting their weaknesses. Let's consider a few examples of companies that developed their response strategy by leveraging this way of thinking.

High on the list is Walmart. How do you respond to a giant like Amazon, the undisputed leader in online retail, responsible for 50 percent of all online sales in the US? On the face of it, Amazon's business model seems unstoppable, but from Walmart's perspective, there is a weakness in it. Whereas Amazon has only 110 warehouses in the US, Walmart has more than 150 distribution centers and 4,789 stores in 49 states. This effectively means that almost every citizen in the US lives within a few miles of a Walmart store. As a result, customers can place online orders and Walmart can use its local stores to distribute these online sales much more quickly and at a much lower shipping cost than Amazon. For example, it has been estimated that the average Amazon order for one-day shipping is $8.32, which costs $10.59 for Amazon to fulfil.[5] Amazon makes healthy margins on orders shipped after more than two days, but when it comes to fast deliveries, Walmart can exploit its decentralized distribution system to be faster and cheaper than Amazon.

In fact, Walmart is gearing up to fight this way. According to an analyst's report: "It turns out Walmart is using its physical stores as warehouses for online sales...That means Walmart will soon have the biggest and most effective 'shipping network' in America. By the end of the year, Walmart plans to deliver stuff from 1,600 stores...Most important, Walmart will pull this off at relatively little cost...Since shipping is the biggest expense in online sales, we are talking a big difference in profits. Walmart will dodge Amazon's fate and save billions on shipping."[6]

Consider another example, TAG Heuer's response to the Apple watch. As described in the previous chapter, the worst thing that TAG Heuer could have done was to try to create a smartwatch to compete with Apple head-on. The company could not beat Apple at its own game, so it had to leverage its strengths and exploit any weaknesses in Apple's approach. As it turned out, the weakness it identified was the fact that Apple could not deliver the emotional benefits of Swiss-made watches that 500 years of mechanical movement expertise could offer. The Apple watch could be sold on its superior functionality, but it is something that the consumer will throw away after a year or two to replace it with one carrying the latest technology. It was, therefore, impossible to create an emotional connection between the watch and the consumer. By contrast, Swiss watches were sold on emotion and the value proposition of "eternity." As the famous Patek Philippe slogan said, a watch is not just a watch, it is something you merely look after for the next generation.

The TAG Heuer response strategy set out to exploit this weakness in the Apple offering. By developing the "modules" approach, the Connected watch offered the consumer both eternity and smartwatch capabilities. You can replace the modules on the watch—maybe use the smartwatch module during the day and the mechanical module in the evening—but you never throw away the watch. You can replace the smartwatch module every year or two, but the mechanical module stays with you for life. At the same time, by maintaining the TAG Heuer brand name as well as its distinct look and feel, and the use of metals that TAG Heuer prided itself on, the company was able to leverage the strength of the brand in its fight with Apple. It is too soon to tell whether the strategy will succeed, but there is no denying its creativity.

A similar strategy was adopted by KBC Bank in Belgium in anticipation of companies like Google and Amazon entering the banking industry. The bank has been ranked repeatedly as the best bank in Europe and its CEO Johan Thijs has been featured on Harvard Business Review's top CEOs of the world list on several occasions. Thijs is in no doubt that companies like Google can use their superior customer data assets and analytical skills to offer customers banking products and services that can match those of any bank in the world. But in his opinion, these Silicon Valley technology companies have one weakness: The customers do not trust them like they trust their local banks. He therefore built his response strategy to exploit Google's weakness. He first built his bank's app to be the digital bank account manager for the customer. Anything that a bank account manager used to do for a customer in the past was now taken over by the app. The customer could ask the app questions as well as request transactions. For example, the app will arrange for your mortgage, or buy your train tickets, or pay for your parking, all through simple voice instructions. The app will also proactively offer solutions based on your past purchases, revealed preferences, and physical location at any given time. As Thijs said: "The app will give you advice and help you on anything that matters to you. It will make your life easier and simpler. In the past, it was your account manager that handled all this. Now you have a digital account manager that resides in your smartphone and goes everywhere you go."

In addition, KBC is aggressively using big data, analytics, and AI to offer customers anything that a big technology company can offer. According to Thijs, the goal is to allow the bank to claim that in financial services, "KBC is good enough in whatever Google can offer you." However, on top of this, he aims to use his bank's advantages over Google to offer the customer products and services that Google cannot offer, such as investment advice and wealth management. These products are not transaction-based, the area where the technology firms have an advantage; they are products that depend on trust and long-term relationships, an area in which local banks such as KBC have an advantage. As Thijs said: "If I try to play the game like Google, I am dead. My goal is to be as good as them in what they do and superior in other areas that I have the advantage."

Yet another example is Nintendo's brilliant response to Microsoft and Sony in the game consoles business. The introduction of Sony's PlayStation and Microsoft's Xbox had transformed the market from one where consoles were viewed as toys, primarily targeting teenage boys with non-violent titles, to one where they became sophisticated technological tools that had to have faster processing speeds and higher-definition graphics, targeting young adults with more sophisticated and more violent games. Unable to compete on these terms, Nintendo sought to exploit the weaknesses in these strategies. The increasing sophistication and violent nature of the games meant that only young adult men were attracted to the industry. As a result, a huge portion of the population, such as women and teenagers, was not catered for. Under the leadership of Satoru Iwata, Nintendo decided to target this customer segment. That led to the development of the Wii, a console that would support simple, real-life games that could be learned quickly and played by all members of the family, including the very youngest and the very oldest. The developers looked beyond technical specifications, creating instead a console that was quiet, used less electricity, and enabled households to play every Nintendo game ever made, rather than having to keep old consoles. By playing simulation games such as tennis, bowling, baseball, and golf, gamers were encouraged to move around and exercise. In short, the Wii was everything that the PlayStation and the Xbox were not. The success of the strategy catapulted Nintendo back to industry leadership.

### Borrow Disruptors' Ideas But Don't Imitate

Disruptions allow for the emergence of opportunities such as new products, services, and customer segments as well as new business models and ways of competing. Many of these may not fit with what we are doing or may be things that we do not have the capabilities or competence to do ourselves. But others may be good new ways of doing business that we can incorporate in our own business model to either improve our competitive position or enable us to partake in the opportunities created by disruption. Therefore, another question that we should raise during the development of our response strategy should be: What ideas and practices can we borrow from the disruptors' strategies and business models to incorporate into our own strategy of response?

Consider how British Airways (BA) responded to the disruption of the low-cost, no-frills, point-to-point business model in the airline industry. This model emerged in the 1970s with Southwest in the US and spread to Europe during the 1980s and 1990s, with easyJet and Ryanair being the main disruptors. The model is based on direct routes to secondary airports on the value proposition of good-enough service and low price. It originally grew by attracting tourists and families but later became good enough to also attract businesspeople on short-haul flights. BA's initial response was to create a separate subsidiary called GO in 1998, to compete in this market by using the same strategy as the disruptors. This strategy did not succeed and GO was purchased in a management buyout in 2001 before being bought by easyJet in 2002. BA had to rethink its response.

The new strategy was to focus on its existing business model, improving even more the quality of service offered to customers (such as dedicated airport lounges, more frequent departures, and a generous air miles program) while at the same time adopting several elements of the disruptive business model. For example, passengers flying economy in continental Europe were quoted the basic economy airfare that did not include the usual frills. If they wanted, they could pay extra for luggage or to reserve a seat. They could also buy food on board. These were all features of the disruptive business model that allowed for the provision of a low price. By adopting them into its own business model, BA was able to do to the disruptors what they originally did to BA themselves. By this I mean that when the disruptors attacked, they did so by claiming: "We are good enough in whatever BA is offering you (i.e. service) and we are superior to them in another area (i.e. price)." What BA did in its response was to say: "I am good enough in what the disruptors are offering you (i.e. price) and I am superior to them in service." By all accounts, the strategy proved to be a big hit for BA.

Consider another example, Sky's response to the disruption of streaming TV. Since its creation in 1989, Sky had built its success on subscription pay TV, growing a loyal and lucrative subscriber base on the back of a strong brand and a great mix of programs. The arrival of streaming TV threatened the viability of the monthly subscription business model. Streaming TV was cheaper than pay TV—on average, minimum spend for pay TV was £45 per month whereas streaming TV was around just £6–£10 per month. In addition, it required no satellite dishes or cable wiring into the house. Streaming TV was also more flexible in that it required customers to sign up for only a month rather than a year as Sky did and made terminating the contract easy. It could also be consumed on TV as well as laptops and mobile devices, and its user interface was perceived as "cooler." It offered different content from Sky—primarily movies and TV series rather than sports—but a significant number of existing Sky customers found it "good enough" relative to Sky content, which many people felt was more than they needed or actually consumed every month. The new competitors such as Netflix and Amazon Prime made good use of data and analytics to offer customers more customized products and to also "nudge" their future purchases based on past purchasing behaviors. New customers, especially the younger generation, were increasingly switching to the new format.

The new way of providing content was growing fast, but it was also presenting a cannibalization threat for Sky's high-margin pay TV offering. Despite this, Sky knew it could not ignore it. It therefore decided to borrow various elements of the new business model to offer a new service, targeting customers who did not already have a pay TV subscription. In 2012 it launched NOW TV in the UK to offer both live streaming and video on demand without a contract. Originally offering only films, it later added sports and entertainment channels. Film and entertainment channels could be accessed through a low monthly fee whereas sports events were accessed on a pay-as-you-go basis. Unlike Sky's flagship satellite TV service, it did not require a long-term contract. The service was slowly rolled out in other European countries such as Germany, Austria, and Italy. It was estimated that by 2019, NOW TV had captured a 10 percent market share in the UK, placing it third behind Netflix and Amazon Prime Video.

Yet another example is how retailers all over the world are borrowing ideas and technologies from digital disruptors to improve the service provided in their stores. For example, in 2018, US grocery chain Kroger introduced digital price tag technology across hundreds of stores. Called "Kroger Edge," it displays pricing and nutritional information digitally, allowing the store to instantly and remotely update the information of each product on the shelf. Similarly, in its Hema store, the first physical store opened by Chinese ecommerce giant Alibaba in 2016, customers can scan

QR codes on products to get more information, including the exact date food items were harvested, sourced, and delivered. Payment can also be made through the Hema app, making shopping quick and convenient. In France, Sephora introduced a virtual artist service in many of its stores. Shoppers can use it to get a "virtual makeover" and test how different makeup will look on them, without actually applying products. At that point, Sephora employees step in to offer shoppers a more professional and customized experience based on technology as well as personal expertise. In China, the supermarket 7Fresh introduced several technology elements to improve the customer's shopping experience. For example, there are several "magic mirrors" in every store that can sense when an item is picked up from the shelf. They immediately display information about that item to help the customer make an educated purchase. Similarly, the store is full of smart shopping carts that do not have to be pushed. Instead, they follow the shopper around the store, allowing customers to keep their hands free for other tasks. Finally, consider Nike's Speed Shop service. Customers can reserve shoes online. They then arrive at the store through a dedicated entrance to find a locker with their name on it which they can unlock with their smartphones. They can try on the shoes and if they like them, pay for them with mobile checkout and depart the store without even standing in line or talking to a human being. These are all examples of how traditional retailers are borrowing ideas and technologies associated with the digital disruption to improve their way of competing.

## Eliminate Things Made Unnecessary by Disruption

Disruption provides incumbents with ideas to improve their business models not only by adding things but also by subtracting things. In fact, innovation is not only discovering new things to offer but also removing things from our offering. Practices and value-chain activities that were once integral parts of the business model may become unnecessary or even value-destroying in the new environment. The third question, therefore, that needs to be asked during the development of a response strategy should be: "What practices or value-chain activities does the disruption enable me to eliminate from my strategy or business model?"

The most obvious candidate for elimination is intermediaries. If there is one thing the digital disruption has allowed for, it is the direct servicing of customers without the middleman. This means, for example, that airline companies like BA can sell directly to customers without the need to go through travel agents. Banks, insurance companies, and brokerage firms can reach customers directly without branches, salespeople, or brokers. Retailers as well as supermarkets can shut many of their shops and shift their sales online. Textbook publishers can distribute their content directly to students' smartphones without the need to go through bookshops. The list is endless.

A good example of this is the NayaMed business model developed by Medtronic.[7] It was set up in 2012 as a separate unit to distribute Medtronic's economy range of heart pacemakers and defibrillators in several European countries, with regional sales and online technical support. NayaMed offered hospitals a new service model composed of an e-commerce platform, which was connected to an RFID inventory solution and a remote technical support system. The online inventory system helped manage stock levels and provided automatic replenishment of goods. More importantly, a remote technical support system based in Lausanne, Switzerland, replaced the onsite presence of a technical rep during implantation and during follow-up sessions by using a box installed in the cath lab that transmitted voice and the video of the programmer. The programmer was based in the hospital. This basically meant that when an implant operation took place, the cath lab technician contacted the NayaMed technical support in Lausanne through the NayaMed instant tech support box and the NayaMed technician walked the lab technician through the procedures to set the parameters of the CRDM device to ensure it was working effectively for the patient. This effectively removed the need for expensive technical reps to be at the hospital during the operation, saving Medtronic millions in costs. An analyst commented on this as follows: "The units are sold only online, not through high-salaried sales representatives. Physician and nurse training and support is no longer in-person, but virtual. Costs are much, much less than in the mainstream business."[8]

It is not only intermediaries that can be removed as a result of disruption. When Netflix moved into streaming of movies, it was able to significantly reduce the distribution of DVDs by post. Admittedly, the switch did not happen as smoothly as Netflix expected, but it got there in the end. Similarly, when Auto Trader Group plc made the transition from being a UK print magazine for people selling their cars to a completely online one, it was able to eliminate all regional magazines and consolidate everything into one national website. The use of social media may also allow for a significant reduction in the organization's advertising budget. For example, it has been estimated[9] that social media will expose you to 1,000 consumers for less than \$3. By contrast, direct mail requires \$57 and broadcast TV \$28. Developing an effective social media campaign can allow for the elimination of traditional media and advertising strategies.

## Innovate How and Where You Compete

As already pointed out several times in this book, disruption should be approached not only as a threat to defend against but also as an opportunity to exploit. For example, disruptive business models do not just cannibalize existing markets, they also create entirely new markets on the periphery of the established markets. Similarly, new technologies destroy existing value chains but also create entirely new ways for companies to compete. This is fertile ground for innovation, and in developing their response strategy, companies should incorporate this way of thinking into their analysis by asking the fourth and final question: "How could we use the disruption to innovate in how or where we compete?"

### DO DIFFERENT THINGS

Innovation can take two forms: We could start doing different things or we could do the same things differently. Consider, first, the idea of doing different things. There is no question that a combination of factors unleashed by the digital disruption is allowing companies to enter markets that they couldn't realistically do just 20 years ago. For example, we have seen Vodafone getting into banking in Africa,[10] Toyota into the design and building of smart cities,[11] Apple into healthcare,[12] Google into retail banking,[13] Amazon into making video games,[14] and Sony experimenting with cars.[15] What enables such unrelated diversification is two things. First, access to customer data. Relative to other more traditional assets such as technology which could be leveraged and used only in markets close to where the technology originated, customer relationships and customer data can be leveraged in markets further afield from the core market. Second, ecosystems and new technologies. Whereas in the past companies had to produce everything themselves and manage their different businesses within one hierarchy, today they can rely on ecosystems that allow them to utilize products and services without having to produce them themselves. They can also use new technology to do today what they could not do before. For example, a company such as Babylon can use AI to offer customized service and advice to patients without having a single doctor on its payroll.

These changes mean that companies can now develop response strategies that allow them to go beyond their core business. A classic example of this is Microsoft. A key pillar of its successful transformation under Nadella since 2014 has been the move into cloud computing. Renting online storage and processing power to big corporate clients has nothing to do with improving the core business of selling (now renting) software. However, it is a clever diversification move that leverages customer relationships among other things. The same could be said of the successful transformation of Axel Springer, the German publishing company, in the last 15 years. The rapid decline of its newspaper and magazine business at the turn of the century meant that its classified ads business was dying. In response, the company moved into the "digital classified ads" business, which in effect meant that it developed online marketplaces that connected buyers with sellers of products such as houses, cars, and job openings. These platforms tend to be winner-take-all businesses, so by moving early Axel Springer was able to corner the market. It created similar platforms in several countries, which allows it to share learning and technology. These platforms now account for the majority of the company's profitability, and the creation of similar marketplaces for other products and services, rather than the legacy business of journalism, is seen as the way to go in the future for the organization.

DO THINGS DIFFERENTLY

The second way in which we can use the disruption to innovate is by doing things differently in our core business. The goal is to go beyond the "borrow" and "eliminate" strategies and identify radical ways to redefine how we compete in the core market. Consider, for example, how farm equipment supplier John Deere is using big data to revolutionize farming. According to one report: "[John Deere] released several products that can connect John Deere's equipment with each other as well as to owners, operators, dealers and agricultural consultants. This interconnectivity helps farmers enhance productivity and increase efficiency. John Deere uses sensors added to their equipment to help farmers manage their fleet and to decrease downtime of their tractors as well as to save on fuel. The information is combined with historical and real-time weather data, soil conditions, crop features and many other data sets. The information is presented in the MyJohnDeere.com platform as well as on the iPad and iPhone app 'Mobile Farm Manager' in order to help farmers figure out what crops to plant where and when, when and where to plough, where the best return will be made with the crops and even which path to follow when ploughing."[16] In short, John Deere has transformed itself from a farm equipment supplier to a provider of farming solutions.

The move away from products to solutions is a common theme in numerous industries. The Swedish conglomerate Assa Abloy has transformed its core business from providing door keys to providing door-opening solutions. The German agriculture machinery manufacturer Claas has transformed itself to become the digital personal assistant of farmers, helping them with connected technologies and data to optimize the operations on their farms. GE created a digital division to develop internet-era cloud software that helps its customers maintain and repair their machines and heavy equipment. Schneider Electric has pivoted from a pure hardware supplier to an energy management provider via an open Internet of Things (IoT) platform. Adobe moved from selling packaged software to offering digital experiences, commerce platforms, and analytics.

Redefining the business from being a provider of a product to being a provider of solutions and services is only one way that we can innovate in the core business. The Dutch bank ING provides another way. Its digital transformation is based on its goal to become a banking platform, connecting buyers and sellers, including offering products of third parties. Leveraging its huge data lake as well as digital technologies, it has been building a platform to become the "go-to place" for customers' finance-related needs. The Belgian bank KBC went one step further. First, through its banking app, it provides customers with a mobile, voice-activated platform to connect them with online shops. In addition, it analyses its vast customer data to develop solutions and offer them to customers before they even know they need them. KBC's goal is to shift from an AI/data-driven organization to a solutions-driven one.

## Innovation Is Key

The framework provided here is only one way to approach the task of developing a strategy of response. The four questions are not the only ones that could be asked, and the organization does not have to base its entire response on the basis of only one of these questions. Using ideas from all four and combining them could lead to an even more effective response. For example, you can "borrow" ideas from the business models of disruptors to improve your business model while at the same time identifying ideas that will attack the weak points in the disruptors' business models. Similarly, you can borrow ideas to improve your ways of playing the game while at the same time eliminating value-chain activities that no longer make sense and simultaneously implementing radical ways to innovate in your approaches. Thus, ideas can flow from all four questions and you should use them to improve your decision making, not to constrain it. There is, however, a key requirement that all the ideas should meet. As already argued in the previous chapter, *the most important characteristic of an effective strategy of response is its innovativeness.* An effective strategy must avoid imitating what others have done in response to the disruption; instead it should help the firm differentiate itself as much as possible. This implies that in answering the four questions, the ideas you should be searching for must be creative and rule breaking.

This naturally raises the question: "How can we enhance our corporate creativity so as to develop innovative ideas for our strategy of response?" This is one of the most researched topics in business, and literally hundreds of ideas, strategies, and frameworks have been proposed to help managers develop innovative strategies or business models.[17] For example, the best-selling book *Blue Ocean Strategy* proposed six analytical techniques that companies can use to develop truly innovative strategies: look across substitute products, across strategic groups, across buyer groups, across complementary products, across the functional–emotional orientation of the industry, and across time.[18] Similarly, another best-selling book, *Competing for the Future*, proposed five mind-opening strategies to explore: escape the tyranny of the served market, redefine what business you are in, search for innovative product concepts, overturn traditional price and performance assumptions, and employ expeditionary marketing.[19] A more recent attempt identified four possible ways to innovate in one's strategy: contradict conventional wisdom, combine products or services that have traditionally been separate, turn limitations, liabilities, or constraints into opportunities, and get ideas from far-flung industries or disciplines.[20] The list could go on and the possibilities are endless. I list 20 additional techniques in Figure 8.2.

FIGURE 8.2  Strategies to help you develop an innovative response strategy

- Use analytical techniques such as the five forces or value curves

- Use open innovation and crowdsourcing

- Redefine what business you are in

- Use analogies

- Take the opposite of accepted assumptions in the industry and build on them

- Use creative recombination techniques

- Question the WHO–WHAT–HOW of your business

- Identify and exploit weaknesses in your rivals' strategies

- Create a positive crisis that will lead to active questioning

- Make your strategy process democratic

- Approach your industry like an entrepreneur or as a new market entrant

- Identify and leverage your core competencies

- Challenge and discard common nonsense beliefs in your industry

- Bring ideas from other industries or disciplines or history

- Identify and overcome constraints in the industry

- Transfer competencies from other parts of the business

- Institutionalize the principle of variety in your strategy process

- Use Edward de Bono's Six Thinking Hats technique

- Adopt the perspective of a stakeholder you like, such as your customer or regulator

- Talk to non-customers or companies in adjacent markets

## The Principle of Variety

With such a plethora of techniques to use, which one or ones should a company choose? The answer is simple enough: It doesn't matter. The key is not to find the "best" technique to use because such a thing does not exist.

Instead, the key is to exploit all of them by *institutionalizing the principle of variety in your strategy process*. This is a mouthful, so let me explain what I mean. First, what is the principle of variety? This simply states that creativity is enhanced when we approach a problem from different angles or different perspectives. This is not rocket science and it's probably something that we all learn from an early age. It is also something that can be applied to any problem we are facing, not just business problems. Edward de Bono's "Six Thinking Hats" technique is one of the most widely known techniques that tries to apply this principle in management.[21] The logic underpinning the principle is that when we develop a dominant way of thinking about something, we become passive thinkers. In other words, we do not think about that issue in an active way and we sleep-walk through any discussion about it. Thus, to "wake up" the brain into active thinking, we need to escape our dominant way of thinking and the best way to do this is by starting our thinking at a new starting point (i.e. a different perspective). Since the brain is not used to thinking in this different way, the very fact that we force it to start from an unfamiliar starting point will make it revert to active thinking. This increases the probability that we will think of new ideas.

### Incorporate Variety in Your Strategy Process

If this is the principle, how do we apply it in our strategy development? Simple. Instead of using just one of the many strategies listed in Figure 8.2, or instead of looking to find the "best" one, it is better to use several of them. The more the better. Every time we switch from one technique to another, we are forcing our brain to start its thinking from a different perspective, and this will encourage more active thinking. While the idea is simple, the reality is that most of us do not apply it. This is why I suggested earlier that this principle should be institutionalized in the strategy process. Something is institutionalized when it becomes part of the culture or processes of the organization so it becomes routine and semi-automatic. As a result, it takes place naturally, without anybody having to think about it. Thus, the strategy process should be designed in such a way that top management is required to go through several of the techniques listed in Figure 8.2 as part of the process. For example, start thinking about your strategy using one of the listed techniques. Once you have developed a few ideas, switch to a totally different approach or technique. Keep doing this until you have used 8–10 of these approaches. To maximize impact, different people could be asked to use different techniques. This way, we will have variety not only in our thinking processes but also in the people doing the thinking.

Improving our strategy development by incorporating the principle of variety in the strategy process is obviously important, but we should not make the mistake of assuming that this alone will be enough to generate innovative strategies. The truth of the matter is that the process of developing superior strategies is part planning, part gut feeling, and part trial and error. It would take a hopelessly romantic planner to argue that analysis alone, however good, is what creates masterful strategies. Similarly, it will be equally silly to pretend that analysis is not necessary, or that intuition and trial and error are enough to give rise to a winning strategy. All three are essential ingredients in the development of a strategy and all three should be made integral parts of our strategy process. We will discuss the importance of experimentation in the next chapter.

## Does Your Strategy Require a New Business Unit?

In developing a response strategy, one of the most important decisions that any organization will have to make is whether to implement its response strategy through a separate unit. This is how many airline companies such as Qantas and Singapore Airlines chose to respond to the low-cost, no-frills business model, and this is how several banks such as Santander and BNP Paribas chose to take advantage of digital banking. This decision will be influenced by several factors. One such factor is top management's assessment of how the established way of doing business will fare in the face of disruption. If top management believes that the established way has no future, then it may be best to create a separate unit to grow the business of the future while allowing the core business to focus on managing its gradual decline. Newspaper companies could be an example of this way of thinking: If you think that the print business is dying a slow death, it may make sense to develop your business of the future through a separate unit. This is not necessarily the only option, and companies such as *The New York Times* in the US and *The Guardian* in the UK have clearly chosen a different strategy. However, a bleak assessment of the future of the core business is certainly one of the key factors that will influence the decision to create a separate unit.

Another factor is the aggressiveness with which a company wants to pursue the market created by disruption. There is no question that creating a separate unit will allow for faster decision making and entrepreneurial behaviors that we don't often see in big, established firms. Thus, the more aggressively it wants to pursue a new market, the more likely it is for a big firm to do it through a separate unit.

Yet another factor that will influence the decision is the presence of conflicts between the existing way of competing in the core market and what is needed to compete in the new market. For example, the new market may grow at the expense of the core market and this will create a cannibalization conflict. Similarly, the new way of competing may undermine the existing distributors and this, in turn, might hurt the core market. The presence of conflicts means that the core business and its managers will often find that the new business model is growing at their expense. They will therefore have incentives to constrain it or even kill it. Creating a separate unit to grow the new market may be a good way to manage the conflicts. By keeping the two business models separate, you prevent the company's existing processes and culture from suffocating the new business model. The new unit can develop its own culture, processes, and strategy without interference from the parent company. It can also manage its business as it sees fit without being suffocated by the managers of the established company who see cannibalization threats and channel conflicts at every turn.

### Connecting to the Core Business

Creating a separate unit will not by itself ensure success. After creating a separate unit, the firm must still find ways to exploit its existing strengths (such as its brand name, financial resources, and industry experience) in the new unit. In this sense, the question that needs to be asked is not "Should we separate or not?" but rather "What activities in our value chain do we separate and what activities do we keep integrated?" There are five areas for which this question needs to be asked:[22]

1 *Location*: Should the separate unit be located close to the parent firm or far away from it?

2 *Name*: Should the separate unit adopt a name similar to the parent name, as United did in naming its separate unit Ted, or should its name be totally different, as BA did in naming its separate unit GO?

3 *Equity*: Should the unit be a wholly-owned subsidiary of the parent or should the parent own only a certain percentage of the equity?

4 *Value-chain activities*: Which value-chain activities should the unit develop on its own and which should it share with the parent? The most common answer to this question is to allow the unit to develop its own

dedicated customer-facing activities and share its back-office activities with the parent. This, however, may not be the appropriate solution for every firm, so this issue has to be considered on a case-by-case basis.

5 *Organizational environment*: Should the unit be allowed to develop its own culture, values, processes, incentives, and people, or should any of these be shared with the parent? Again, the most common solution is to allow the unit to develop its own culture but unite the parent and the unit through the adoption of common shared values. This, however, may not be appropriate for every firm, so again this is something that needs to be considered on a case-by-case basis.

## Ensure the New Business Has a Unique Strategy

Besides deciding what activities to separate and what to keep the same, the firm must decide what strategy the new unit should adopt. It is imperative that the parent avoids "exporting" the strategy of the core business to the new unit. While the desire to transfer the firm's strengths, competencies, and knowledge to the new unit is understandable, this should not be taken to imply that the strategy of the core business must also be transferred to the new unit. It sounds surprising, but many established firms have made this mistake. It is easy to think that the market being created by disruption is simply an extension of the established market. After all, what is the difference between the low end of the airline market and the established market? Aren't they simply two segments of the same market? If firms start their thinking this way, they will naturally approach entry into the new market as a lateral move from their established market. Thus, rather than attempt entry like an entrepreneur with a clean slate, they will become preoccupied with how to leverage their existing assets in the new market. Rather than start out with the realities of the new market and work backward to design a strategy appropriate for it, they will start with what they have in the established market and attempt to transfer it into the new market. As a result, they will often imitate their disruptors' successful business model and try to outcompete them using their existing strengths.

To be successful, firms need to be alert enough to appreciate that even though the new market *appears* similar to the established market, this is nothing but an illusion. They should therefore approach the new market like an entrepreneur by asking themselves: "If I were to enter this new market, what strategy should I adopt?" Rather than focus on defending their existing market, their goal should be to attack the new market. And since we know from research that new market entry almost always ends up in failure unless the attacker adopts an innovative business model, established firms that enter the new markets by adopting a radical new strategy will have a higher chance of being successful.[23]

## Will Your New Strategy Work?

In 1988, Jean Paul Gaillard left Philip Morris to join Nespresso as its commercial director. Nestlé had been doing research on the concept of Nespresso since 1976. It finally tested the new product in Japan in 1986 and introduced it in the Swiss market that same year. It turned out to be a big flop. Quarter after quarter, sales were significantly below target, and no effort by top management to rejuvenate its fortunes seemed to work. It soon developed a bad reputation in the market and people within Nestlé started referring to it as a "black hole"—you throw money into it and nothing comes out. The situation was so bad that Nestlé decided to terminate the new product just a few weeks after Gaillard joined Nespresso.[24] This came as a big surprise to Gaillard, but rather than give up in frustration, he asked his bosses for some additional time to develop and try a new strategy for Nespresso. The rest, as they say, is history. Gaillard changed in a radical way the original market positioning and strategy of Nespresso and set it upon a path of tremendous growth and profitability. Today, it is one of the strongest brands in the Nestlé portfolio and one of its most profitable units.

There is no question that the strategy developed by Gaillard was a radical break from Nespresso's original strategy. For example, he changed the positioning of Nespresso from mass market to luxury. He changed the distribution of the coffee machines from home-appliance stores to high-end retailers such as Harrods and Bloomingdale's. He changed the distribution of coffee capsules from supermarkets to the Nespresso Club. He changed the targeted customer from offices to individuals. He separated the machine side of the business from the coffee side and subcontracted the machine side to OEMs such as Krupps and Philips. We all know now that the new strategy turned out to be a big success, but at the time of introduction it must have looked like a big gamble. What gave Gaillard the confidence to implement it? More importantly, what gave Nestlé the confidence to invest in it?

In Gaillard's own words: "You can do market research to check your ideas, but my belief is that market research is not particularly effective when it comes to truly new things. Market research is useful but only for checking things that already exist. Consumers can only give you meaningful feedback on what they already know. For truly innovative things, you are better off testing them on the market. So, to make sure that my ideas were fine, we tried a few of them in a limited way to make sure they worked. For example, my proposal to change our targeted customer from offices to individuals was resisted by top management. I therefore said: 'Fine, let's try this one out.' We went to two home appliance outlets in Geneva, two more in Lausanne, and another one in Nyon, and we started selling Nespresso machines to individual consumers. My goal was to try this out for a week and deliver a high enough target so that top management would take notice. It did not take a week for us to see the individual consumer responding to our offer enthusiastically."

This anecdote highlights the key challenge that faces any organization with a new strategy. Specifically, how do you know if your strategy is a good one and how do you convince the rest of the organization to follow you? This is especially the case for truly innovative strategies. As we have argued repeatedly in this chapter, an effective response strategy must avoid imitating what others have done in response to the disruption and should instead help the firm differentiate itself as much as possible. In other words, it should be an innovative strategy. Imagine that you have succeeded in developing such an innovative strategy. Your task now is to assess whether it's any good and convince the rest of the organization to follow you. How do you do that? As the Nespresso example highlights, experimentation can be an effective way to both test a new strategy and convince others to accept it. This much is true, but what people forget is that there are good experiments and there are stupid experiments. How do you make sure you design and carry out a clever experiment, especially when it comes to trying out a new strategy? We turn to this topic next.

# References

1   Willy Shih: "The real lessons from Kodak's decline," *Sloan Management Review*, Summer 2016, pp. 10–13; Scott Anthony: "Kodak's downfall wasn't about technology," *Harvard Business Review*, digital edition, July 15, 2016; Chunka Mui: "How Kodak failed," *Forbes*, January 18, 2012.

**2**  Greg Satell: "How Blockbuster, Kodak and Xerox really failed (It's not what you think)," *Inc*, July 7, 2018.

**3**  Stephen McBride: "Walmart has made a genius move to beat Amazon," Forbes, January 8, 2020.

**4**  Jack Ewing: "The car industry is under siege," *The New York Times*, June 6, 2019.

**5**  Karen Weise: "Amazon's profit falls sharply as company buys growth," *The New York Times*, October 24, 2019.

**6**  Stephen McBride: "Walmart has made a genius move to beat Amazon," *Forbes*, January 8, 2020.

**7**  This account is based on the case study by Daniel Oyon, Costas Markides, and Lisa Duke: "NayaMed (A)," London Business School, 2015.

**8**  Stephen Wunker: "Five approaches when you need costovation, not innovation," *Forbes*, December 10, 2013.

**9**  "US ad spending by media," *eMarketer*, August 2013.

**10**  Nic Fildes and Tom Wilson: "Vodafone targets Africa's unbanked with ambitious plans for M-Pesa," *Financial Times*, December 18, 2019.

**11**  "Toyota to build 'city of the future' at the base of Mount Fuji," *The Japan Times*, January 7, 2020.

**12**  Tatiana Darie: "Apple's healthcare take could be $313 billion by 2027, analysts say," *Fortune*, April 8, 2019.

**13**  Tim Bradshaw and Robert Armstrong: "Google in talks to move into banking," *Financial Times*, November 13, 2019.

**14**  Seth Schiesel: "Amazon pushes into making video games, not just streaming their play," *The New York Times*, April 2, 2020.

**15**  Patrick Lucas Austin: "Sony showed up to CES with a radically different concept car. A top executive told us why," *TIME*, January 14, 2020.

**16**  Mark van Rijmenam: "John Deere is revolutionizing farming with big data," *Datafloq*, February 21, 2013.

**17**  A new and intriguing technique recently developed is based on leveraging your own or your rivals' mistaken beliefs. See the work of Jules Goddard, Julian Birkinshaw, and Tony Eccles: "Uncommon sense: How to turn distinctive beliefs into action," *Sloan Management Review*, Spring 2012, Vol. 53, No. 3, pp. 32–39.

**18**  Chan Kim and Renee Mauborgne: *Blue Ocean Strategy*, Boston, MA: HBS Press, 2005.

**19**  Gary Hamel and CK Prahalad: *Competing for the Future*, Boston, MA: HBS Press, 1994.

**20**  Adam Brandenburger: "Strategy needs creativity," *Harvard Business Review*, March–April 2019, pp. 2–9.

**21**  Edward de Bono: *Six Thinking Hats*, London: Penguin Life, 2016.

22  Ranjay Gulati and Jason Garino: "Get the right mix of bricks and clicks," *Harvard Business Review*, May–June 2000, pp. 107–114.

23  See for example Paul Geroski: "What do we know about entry?" *International Journal of Industrial Organization*, 1995, Vol. 13, pp. 421–440; Paul Geroski: *Market Dynamics and Entry*, Oxford, UK: Basil Blackwell, 1991.

24  Costas Markides and Daniel Oyon: "Changing the strategy at Nespresso: An interview with former CEO Jean Paul Gaillard," *European Management Journal*, 2000, Vol. 18, No. 3, pp. 296–301.

# 09

# Test Your Strategy of Response

## *How to Experiment in a Clever Way*

An effective strategy of response must allow the firm to not only defend against the disruption but also exploit it. The goal should be to take advantage of the changes brought about by the disruption in order to reposition and differentiate the firm in the new industry environment. Once such a strategy is developed, the challenge becomes how to convince our people that this is the correct response for us. In addition, no strategy will be perfect from the start, so we need to ensure that we learn from the market and adjust what we are doing accordingly. How do you know if your strategy is right and how do you convince others to support you? A good way to achieve both objectives is through experimentation. Rather than debate endlessly whether an idea is good or bad, why not try it out in the market in a quick and low-cost way to see if it works or not? This is not a controversial suggestion because the benefits of experimentation are many and well known. However, the truth of the matter is that some experiments are better than others. What is the difference between a clever experiment and a not-so-clever one? We can answer this question by examining two examples—one of a good experiment and one of a bad experiment.

## Example #1: easyCinema

In May 2003, Stelios Haji-Ioannou, the founder of easyJet, launched a new venture called easyCinema. The company aimed to turn the cinema business on its head, the way easyJet did in the airline business. Starting with the premise that on average only one in five theater seats was sold for a given screening, and that the cost of going to the movies was too high, a new business model was developed. This model utilized dynamic pricing to determine the price of a ticket based on factors that influenced the demand for a movie, such as its popularity, the day and time at which the customer wanted to go see the movie, and time since its release. As a result, the company was able to offer screenings for as little as 20 pence when the average ticket price for a movie in London was £10 plus an additional £8 for popcorn and cola. It was not known what the maximum price of the ticket would be, but it was believed to be lower than £5. In addition, the easyCinema theaters were designed to be low-cost operations. For example, they had no ticket counters. The customer purchased the ticket online, printed a receipt, and used the barcode on the receipt to gain access to the theater. Furthermore, the cinemas had no employees available to help customers. No drinks or ice cream or popcorn were available for sale, but the customers were encouraged to bring their own if they wanted. At the end of a movie, the company encouraged customers to clean up after themselves, very much like they did on easyJet flights.

The new business model was radical and unconventional, and the company decided to try it out first in a limited way before launching it on the market. For the initial experiment, a multiplex 10-screen theater was identified in the small city of Milton Keynes, one hour north of London. The company leased it for three years and converted it into an easyCinema. The new venture initially struggled to gain access to the big movies because major distributors were not prepared to release new films to a company using the yield-management model. However, it was able to start operations by screening movies by independent producers. The new cinema received national and international attention, and several TV networks dedicated significant airtime to discussing it. On launch day, TV crews from eight countries, including Japan and the US, were present to report on it. Stelios Haji-Ioannou himself spent a lot of time appearing on news programs and giving newspaper interviews, promoting the new service.

The experiment ran for three years. In the first few months, it attracted huge crowds, but the initial enthusiasm was not sustained, even though the company succeeded in gaining access to first-run films for a fixed price. The company also relented on not serving popcorn and drinks, but that was not enough to reverse the decline in attendance. The cinema closed in May 2006 and no further attempts were made to relaunch it elsewhere by building on the learning acquired through the experiment. Perhaps *that* was the learning, that it was not a good concept and that it should be terminated. However, this was not what Stelios Haji-Ioannou was saying at the time of closure. Instead, he was complaining about the major distributors who refused to release their movies to him and hinted that he might take legal action against them. He also commented that it might have been better to have run the experiment in London rather than the small town of Milton Keynes.

What can we learn from this experience? easyCinema experimented with its strategy before investing huge resources in it and our task is to evaluate whether the experiment was a good one. Undertaking an experiment is exactly what all of us have been recommending to companies. Specifically, we advise companies to experiment with their new strategy and use any learning to improve it before investing huge resources in its implementation. If we learn through the experiment that the strategy is destined for failure, so be it. We discard it and move on. At least we will have saved ourselves a lot of money and a lot of heartache. In this sense, we cannot use the "failure" of the easyCinema experiment as evidence that the experiment was not a good one. Maybe the experiment did its job in informing us that the easy-Cinema business model was not a viable one. Therefore, how can we assess whether the experiment was a good one, irrespective of the final outcome?

## Was It a Good Experiment?

The answer is that it *is* possible to evaluate how good an experiment is without knowing its outcome, and in the case of easyCinema, the experiment was a bad one. To appreciate why this is the case, let's undertake a thought experiment. Imagine that you run this experiment and the outcome after six months is total failure: Nobody is interested in coming to your theaters to watch a movie, even at a price of 20 pence. You therefore sit down with your management team to try to understand the reasons for the failure. You ask your team to give you their assessment. One says that in his opinion, the failure can be attributed to the location. For a number of reasons, the small town of Milton Keynes is not the right place to try this new concept. At that point, somebody else jumps into the discussion to disagree with this assessment. She argues that the failure had nothing to do with the location but was down to the "product." Going to the cinema is an experience and we have taken that away from people. If they wanted to watch a movie at a low cost, they could do it at home by watching a DVD. Just then, another manager jumps in to offer her opinion. She argues that neither of the two factors already mentioned is the real reason for our failure to attract customers. In her opinion, the real reason is the fact we could not offer people the blockbuster movies that the major studios were producing. Needless to say, this discussion can go on for a long time. The point is: Do we know which of these managers is correct? Do we know which of these factors are the real reasons for the failure? Not really. They could all be correct, or they could all be wrong and another, unmentioned reason is the real cause for our failure. Therefore, we have just run an experiment to learn something and what have we learned? Nothing.

How about if the outcome of the experiment was not total failure but a great success? Imagine this outcome and you again sit down with your management team to assess why you were so successful. You ask your team to give you their assessments. One says it's the really low price that attracted the customers; another says it is the novelty of the experience; someone else jumps in and argues that the location made the difference—unlike central London, Milton Keynes is full of customers who are hungry for a low-cost offering; yet somebody else thinks it's the unconventional movies we are screening. Again, this can go on forever, but consider the same questions as before: Do we know which of these managers is correct? Do we know which of these factors are the real reasons for the success? Not really. We have just run an experiment to learn something and ended up learning nothing.

One might argue that this is being too harsh on the experiment. What does it matter if we don't know the specific reasons for its failure or success? Isn't the purpose to learn whether something works or not, no matter what the specific factors are? The answer to this is yes and no. Yes, we want to find out if something works or not, but we also need to know *why* it works or not. Even if it works well, there may be elements that could be improved, so we need to know which ones. Even if it fails, it may be because of one or two things in it that need improvement. Once we improve them or change them, the business model may work just fine. It will be a shame to throw it away without giving it a chance to improve itself. Therefore, the purpose of the experiment is not only to make a yes or no decision, but to also learn about the various components of the business model and improve it. Besides, the outcome may just be a function of luck. If this is the case, we may be throwing away a perfectly good business model or we may be investing in a business model that will soon start delivering bad results. We need to understand *why* we got the specific outcome in order to make an intelligent decision on how to proceed.

So, what was the problem with this experiment and why did we end up learning nothing about why the easyCinema concept did not work? The answer is obvious to anybody who has ever run a scientific experiment in a laboratory: There are too many variables that vary (that is, they are not constant) during the experiment, all of which may affect the outcome. As a result, we cannot know which of these variables are important and which are not. Let's try to understand what this means in the context of the easy-Cinema experiment. As with any new business model, there are many uncertainties in the easyCinema concept. For example, will enough customers find the value proposition of cheap movies without any frills attractive enough? Can we get the major studios and distributors to rent their major movies to us? Will it make a difference if we offer popcorn and drinks? Will a starting price of 99 pence have as much of a wow factor as our price of 20 pence? Can we staff the cinema with a few people without incurring prohibiting costs? Is the concept more attractive in wealthy and cosmopolitan London or in smaller and less wealthy cities? We don't really know the answers to these questions and the purpose is to run the experiment to find out. Granted, some of these uncertainties can be resolved with basic market research, but no amount of market research will eliminate all uncertainties. The problem is that if we run an experiment with all these uncertainties present in the model, we will not know what caused the final outcome. Was it the location, or maybe the price, or perhaps the service and the product offered? We cannot possibly know on the basis of just one experiment.

What is the solution to this problem? One possibility is to first make a list of all the major uncertainties in the business model. The best way to identify major uncertainties is to take note of those topics or issues that generate the most heated discussions and disagreements among top management. For example, if top management cannot agree whether the easyCinema business model is particularly suited for London or Milton Keynes, you know that location is a major uncertainty you need to resolve. Once you generate the list, identify which of these uncertainties can be resolved through market research rather than through experimentation. For example, you do not need an experiment to find out if the major distributors will be willing to rent their movies to you. This is something you can determine by talking with them. Eliminating uncertainties through market research is important because each of the remaining uncertainties will require a dedicated experiment to resolve it. Having too many uncertainties will mean having to run too many experiments and this could be costly. Once you have narrowed down the number of uncertainties to just a few, you then design a series of experiments, each of which focuses on one uncertainty. Keeping all other uncertainties constant, you run one experiment with the uncertainty you are exploring at one level and then again at another level. For example, if you aim to test whether location is important, you run the easyCinema experiment in London and then again in Milton Keynes. Any difference in outcome can only be attributed to the choice of location. Similarly, if the uncertainty you are exploring is the provision of popcorn and drinks, you should run the experiment without popcorn and drinks and then repeat the experiment in the same location with popcorn and drinks. Again, any difference in outcome can be directly linked to this uncertainty.

I mentioned above that this is one way to solve the problem of too many variables varying at the same time in any experiment and now you can understand why. This approach will require the running of multiple experiments to resolve every uncertainty one by one. This can prove expensive and time consuming, and may even confuse customers. There are, of course, ways to manage these problems—for example, easyCinema could use each of its ten screens as a different site for an experiment and could run experiments simultaneously to save time. Alternatively, you could choose to run experiments in geographic areas that are far from your own market so as not to confuse customers or damage the brand if the experiment fails. This is what Adobe chose to do when it was contemplating whether to switch its business model to a subscription model: It tested the subscription model in Australia, far from its core business in the US. However, there is no question that the strategy of running multiple experiments to test each uncertainty one by one is expensive and time consuming. Is there an alternative way to undertake an experiment? Let's consider the case of Rent the Runway.

## Example #2: Rent the Runway

Rent the Runway (RTR) was started by two Harvard Business School classmates, Jennifer Hyman and Jennifer Fleiss, in November 2009. RTR rents designer dresses for either four or eight days at a small fraction of the retail price of the dress, through its platform RTR Reserve. It also offers monthly subscription options. Each dress rental comes with a back-up size at no extra cost to ensure it fits. The rental price includes the dry cleaning and care of the garments. The company also rents children's clothes, as well as accessories such as bags and jewelry, and sells essentials such as tights and cosmetics. In addition to the online business, it has five physical locations in New York, Washington D.C., Chicago, Los Angeles, and San Francisco. Customers can visit any of the stores for advice or to rent. Customers can also reserve dresses well in advance. At its last round of financing in March 2019, the company was valued in excess of $1 billion.

The business model was based on the premise that women will be willing to rent rather than buy designer dresses.[1] This, in turn, depended on designers supporting the idea and being willing to "allow" their dresses to be rented. To them, renting dresses at a fraction of the retail price sounded like a huge cannibalization risk for their lucrative business of selling them through department stores. They could not really prevent someone from buying the dresses and then renting them out, but the new company did not want to go into business with the major designers bad-mouthing or not supporting the venture. As a result, the two founders decided to test the waters before starting anything. They first approached Diane von Furstenberg, an influential fashion designer, to seek her views on their idea. Their original plan was not to rent the dresses themselves. Instead, the designers would undertake to rent through their websites and RTR would manage warehouse and customer service operations for a fee. The frosty reception that this idea received from Furstenberg led the founders to revise their plan and go for the current model whereby RTR buys and rents the dresses itself. Meetings with other designers allowed the founders to make additional changes to the model they had in mind. For example, they had originally planned to target older women who had been exposed to designer clothes and who had purchasing power. After talking to designers, they realized that doing so would create the biggest retail cannibalization risk. They therefore decided to focus on younger women. These women would not normally buy designer dresses, but by renting to them, the designers would expose them to their brand and make them future buyers. Similarly, the founders' original intention was not to buy the dresses outright but to borrow them from designers through a profit-sharing arrangement. This idea was abandoned when it became clear that designers preferred a straightforward purchase by RTR.

One big uncertainty in the concept was whether women would be willing to rent dresses. To assess the appetite for that, the two founders invited 140 Harvard University students to a "styling event" in a Harvard dormitory. During this trial, the 125 women that showed up were given the choice of 130 dresses from 15 designers at prices ranging between $35 to $75. The women were encouraged to try on the dresses and to ask for styling advice. At the end of the day, 34 percent of them decided to rent a dress. This trial demonstrated that women would rent dresses, but would they do so if they did not have the opportunity to try them on first? To test this, the founders organized another trial, at Yale University, where the students could view the dresses but could not try them on. Of the women that showed up, 75 percent decided to rent a dress, supporting the notion that women will rent without trying. In both the Harvard and the Yale trials, the women were given pre-addressed return envelopes to mail the dresses back. The aim was to test whether returning the dresses through the post was a viable option. In fact, all dresses were returned within two days and only two had minor stains. Finally, to assess whether women would buy online, 1,000 women were emailed PDFs with pictures of dresses that they could rent by phone. Even though only 5 percent of them rented a dress, this figure was above the target rate that was required for a profitable service.

Encouraged by the results, the founders secured financing and prepared to launch. One week before its official launch, the company tested a beta version of its service with about 5,000 invited members. The test allowed RTR to see that customers had numerous questions about the company and needed styling guidance. As a result, it beefed up its customer service team to handle questions and requests. When it launched in November 2009, RTR had only 800 dresses from 30 designers in stock. The idea was to use the minimum viable product approach[2] to start the business and scale up once the concept was proven successful. At the beginning, the company allowed for department stores to have an exclusive selling window of several weeks before RTR would offer the same dresses for rent. The purpose was to minimize cannibalization. However, data collected in the first few months of operation showed that the opportunity for additional sales at retail shops was far bigger than any cannibalization risk. Based on this data, the majority of designers abandoned their demand for an exclusive selling window for department stores. In addition, customer feedback in those early stages led RTR to redesign the website's welcome pages and the checkout process.

## Clever Experimentation

So, what can we learn from RTR's experience about "clever" experimentation?[3] First, in order to decide what experiments to run, you need to specify in advance what are the things you want to learn about. In other words, what are the uncertainties in the business model or the hidden assumptions in your thinking? The worst thing you can do is to run an experiment hoping to learn something without being clear in advance exactly what it is you need to learn about. Identifying the uncertainties in the business model should not be that difficult and there are several strategies that you can use to do so. One is to brainstorm with the management team and list the issues that generate the most heated debates and disagreements among your team members. Another way is to talk to potential customers, suppliers, investors, or other stakeholders and identify the issues that worry them the most. Yet another way is to use analytical techniques. A good one that can help in identifying hidden assumptions is discovery-driven planning.[4] Whatever method you adopt, the goal is to identify the major uncertainties in the business model that need to be resolved before you can implement it. Having identified key uncertainties, the next question to explore is: "Which of these uncertainties could be resolved through market research?" For example, one uncertainty in the RTR business model that was resolved by talking with designers was the issue of buying as opposed to renting the dresses from them. Another one was whether they should target older rather than younger women. Yet another was whether the RTR team needed to do the renting of the dresses themselves or whether the designers could do this and RTR would support them. Resolving uncertainties through market research is important because it reduces the number of experiments that need to be run later on.

Market research will not eliminate all uncertainties. At this point, a series of experiments needs to be designed to test one uncertainty at a time. The example of RTR highlights this point well. Unlike easyCinema, RTR did not undertake just one experiment that tested the whole business model in one go. Instead, it ran multiple experiments, each one limited in scope, low-cost, and quick. Each experiment tested individual components of the business model: Will women rent dresses? Will they rent them without trying them on? Will they rent them online? If you remember, this is exactly the same process that Gaillard followed in testing the new strategy of Nespresso. Instead of testing the whole strategy in one go, he tested individual components—for example, he assessed whether individuals rather than offices should be the targeted customer through a series of experiments in five retailers, over one week. Trying to test the whole business model makes learning difficult because too many variables (i.e. components of the business model) vary at the same time.

Once most of the uncertainties are resolved, you will have a business model that you may consider ready for launch. It is only at this point that you may want to run one final experiment to test the whole business model. The idea is to see whether you missed anything or whether any unintended consequences emerge. For example, RTR ran a beta version of its service one week before launch and in the process discovered that it had to beef up its customer service capability. The launch itself should be considered as another experiment in the learning process. You therefore start it small and low-cost to see if it works according to plan. The first few months of operations are also valuable learning opportunities. For example, RTR kept collecting data after launch and tested whether it was necessary to give department stores an exclusive selling window. When the data showed that the opportunity for additional sales at retail shops was far bigger than any cannibalization risk, the exclusive selling window was abandoned. In short, experimentation does not have to end with the launch of the new strategy. It should be part of the day-to-day operations of the firm and should be the preferred method for deciding on any new things the firm wants to do in its markets.

## It Is Difficult to Get People to Experiment

Conducting an experiment the "correct" way is one thing. Creating a culture of experimentation in the organization is another. As we argued in Chapter 4, our agility will be enhanced if we create a culture or an organizational environment that encourages every employee to experiment within clear and explicit strategic parameters set by top management. Obviously, the average employee will not be expected to experiment with our strategy of response as described above because the decision on what strategy to adopt lies outside these parameters and outside their sphere of responsibility. However, numerous other decisions will likely fall within these parameters and it is important that people know not only how to conduct experiments the proper way but also that this is the desired thing to do. As already discussed, employees will not experiment unless we first create a supportive organizational environment around them that supports experimentation. However, people's preference for analysis and rational arguments is so ingrained in our educational systems and in our national cultures that creating a supportive organizational environment for experimentation will not be enough. It is necessary but not sufficient.

The best way to illustrate the nature of the problem we are facing is through one of the most famous puzzles in mathematics, known as the gold or goats puzzle, or the stick or switch puzzle.[5] It goes like this: You are facing three doors. Behind one door, there is a lot of gold. Behind the other two doors, there are goats. You pick one door randomly, hoping to win the gold. Obviously, the probability that you picked the door with the gold behind it is one out of three. At that point, I open one of the other doors that's hiding a goat. I then give you a choice: Do you want to stick to your original choice, or do you want to switch to the other unopened door? What will *you* choose? Unsurprisingly, the majority of people choose to stick to their original choice. I have been trying this puzzle with my students for 30 years now and I'd say that about 85 percent of them choose to stick. To them, the logic is simple: There are two doors left and either could be hiding the gold, so it doesn't matter whether they stick or switch. Either door is facing a 50/50 proposition. Since it doesn't matter, they prefer to stick to their original choice because if they switch and lose out, they would be upset. This all sounds perfectly logical, but the correct answer is actually the opposite one—the optimal strategy is to switch. Why? Because the probability of winning the gold by sticking is one out of three whereas if you switch, the probability of winning is two out of three. There is a very counterintuitive reason for this answer, so it will not help if I try to explain it. However, this is not the reason I mention this puzzle here. The real reason is to tell you of two other things that happen after we try this puzzle in class.

First, before we give the correct answer to the students, we ask them to spend some time convincing their classmates that their approach is the right one. Basically, we first ask all those who chose the stick option to convince the switch people that sticking is the right strategy. Once they spend half an hour trying to do this, we then give the switch people the same opportunity and time to convince everybody else that switching is the better strategy. Over 30 years, with thousands of subjects involved, we have never had a single person succeed in convincing anybody else. Zero. That is quite amazing and highlights how counterintuitive the logic of the puzzle is. No matter what argument people use or what logic they employ, they simply cannot persuade their colleagues that the probabilities are anything other than 50/50. At that point, we ask the students whether other than rational arguments, there is another way to convince people. Quite quickly, they settle on experimentation—why don't we try this a few times to see what we can learn? We therefore split them into teams and ask them to spend a while trying out this puzzle a few times. We ask them to make at least 50 attempts and then report back how many times the stick strategy wins and how many times the switch strategy wins. Predictably, team after team reports that the switch strategy wins most of the time. Sure, the stick strategy wins the gold in some trials, but the difference in probabilities is so big (one out of three versus two out of three) that if you try the puzzle enough times, the switch strategy will win in most of the trials. It is quite impressive to be in a room with 15 or 20 teams when one by one they report which strategy won the experiment. In most cases, all 15 teams report that switch is the winning strategy. Every now and then, you have a team where the stick strategy wins in the majority of trials, but even in that case it is 1 versus 14 teams. The superior strategy is clear for all to see.

This, of course, illustrates the importance of experimentation in convincing other people about an idea. The more counterintuitive or unconventional your idea, the more difficult it is to sell it to your colleagues and convince them to adopt it. But nobody can argue with data. A good experiment allows you to collect the data that will, in turn, allow you to sell your idea. But here's what I find the most interesting lesson from this puzzle. After using this exercise to illustrate to the students the importance of experimentation, we then give them a series of problems to solve.[6] Sometimes the problems are assigned on the same day we ran the stick-or-switch puzzle and sometimes over the following two weeks. All of them are specifically selected problems whose solutions are more easily obtained through experimentation. Guess what? Almost never do the students use experimentation to solve them. Even after they are given indirect hints to "use the learning from the stick-or-switch puzzle" to tackle these new problems, students still try to solve them through analysis or discussion. It's as if people have a natural dislike for experimentation!

This suggests that it is particularly difficult to get people to adopt an experimentation mindset. There may be lots of reasons for this, such as fear of failure, an education system that is biased toward thinking and analysis, resource constraints, or time pressures. There is no question that creating an organizational environment that supports and promotes experimentation can help, but given how many factors work against it, we may have to do something more than creating the environment for it. In fact, we have to do two things. First, we need to "institutionalize" the behavior of experimentation in the fabric of the organization. By this I mean that we need to embed it not only in the culture but also in the processes and systems of the organization. This is exactly what we said in the last chapter when we talked about the need to embed the principle of variety in our strategy process. In a similar fashion, the behavior of experimentation should be made part of the strategy and evaluation processes of the firm and part of the day-to-day conversations in the corridors. The second thing we need to do is *make experimentation a habit* for our employees, a routine part of their working life and something that happens in a non-thinking, semi-automatic manner.[7] Something becomes semi-automatic because we have done it so many times that we can now do it without thinking. Consider, for example, how much active thinking you had to do when you were learning to drive a car and how little active thinking goes into it now, after years of practice. To help our employees develop the habit of experimentation, we need to encourage them to start their learning by undertaking small experiments at first, making sure that every experiment is a rewarding experience. Once they undertake several experiments in their careers, the activity ought to become more natural and routine over time. Having kickstarted the process like this, we can then build the supportive organizational environment in order to sustain the momentum. It is the combination of these two actions with a supportive organizational environment that will help our people develop the experimentation mindset and overcome the bias for analysis that our educational system creates in all of us over the first 20 years of our lives.

# References

1   The account presented here is based on the Harvard Business School case study by Thomas Eisenmann and Laura Winig: "Rent the Runway," case number 9-812-077, Rev: December 17, 2012.

2   The concept of minimum viable product is from Eric Ries: *The Lean Startup*, New York: Crown Business, 2011.

3   Our treatment of experimentation here will be by necessity short and will focus primarily on how to experiment with strategy (rather than products or ideas). There is a rich literature on how to conduct clever business experiments; interested readers are encouraged to read the work of Stefan Thomke, in particular: Stefan Thomke: *Experimentation Matters*, Boston, MA: HBR Press, 2003, as well as Stefan Thomke and Jim Manzi: "The discipline of business experimentation," *Harvard Business Review*, December 2014, and Eric Anderson and Duncan Simester: "A step-by-step guide to smart business experiments," *Harvard Business Review*, March 2011.

4   Rita Gunther MacGrath and Ian MacMillan: "Discovery driven planning," *Harvard Business Review*, July–August 1995, pp. 44–54.

5   Tim Hartford: "Monty Hall and the game show stick-or-switch onion puzzle," *Financial Times*, October 6, 2017.

6  For example, here's one which is based on Russian roulette: You have a gun with six chambers. There are three bullets in the gun, all arranged in consecutive order. You will play Russian roulette with this gun and you can choose from two options. In the first option, you spin the cylinder and then put the gun to your head and pull the trigger. You then spin the cylinder again and shoot a second time. You spin the cylinder one last time and shoot again. In the second option, you spin the cylinder and then put the gun to your head. You then shoot three times in a row without spinning the chamber again. What option do you prefer? If you are good with probabilities, you will likely come up with the right answer quickly. But evidence shows that most people prefer option one, which is the wrong one. A quick experiment will enable you to see why this is the wrong option more clearly.

7  Ko Kuwabara: "Building success habits: Networking and the science of self-change," Columbia Business School, case ID#CU189, September 28, 2017.

# 10

# Implement Your New Strategy

## *How to Make the Transition*

Transitioning from one strategy to another is always difficult, but some transitions are more difficult and more time consuming than others. There are reasons for this and it's important to understand what they are and how to manage them. Consider, for example, the contrasting fortunes of two organizations that undertook a radical change of strategy at about the same time.

The first is Auto Trader Group plc. The company is the UK's number one online marketplace for car buyers, with more than 11 million unique users every month. It started life in 1977 as a print magazine featuring classified advertisements. The magazine was published weekly in 12 regional editions. The need for regional editions was obvious: A national magazine would require thousands of pages to list all cars being advertised. In addition, consumers were searching for cars in their local communities and visited their regional dealers. The company was quick to recognize the potential of the internet and took the first step toward a digital transformation in 1996, with the creation of a separate unit, Autotrader Online. The unit was based in London and was given the task to move the company's products, distribution, and operations online. The original team of 20 were all new recruits from outside the core business, often described by core managers as "young and arrogant." They were given key performance indicators (KPIs) that were totally different from those used in the print business and they embarked on building the online business with a start-up mentality, avoiding any conduct with the parent company. Print circulation at the time was around 350,000 copies a week.

Over time, the online business grew while the print business shrank. As one senior executive put it: "The budget of the print side of the business got reduced every day; the attention it received got reduced every day; its head-count got reduced every day." By 2012, print circulation dropped to an average of 87,000 copies a week, falling to 27,000 by March 2013. In June 2013, after 36 years, Auto Trader printed the last editions of the magazine and moved to focus solely on digital products. The transition from print to digital took 17 years (1996–2013). By all accounts, it was a dramatic and successful transformation. The company went public in 2015 with a market cap of around £2 billion. It has since increased its market value to an esti-mated £4.84 billion by May 2020.

Consider now the case of Nestlé. Around the same time that Auto Trader was taking the first steps in its transformation, Peter Brabeck was appointed CEO of the Swiss-based multinational. He remained as CEO for 12 years (1997–2008), during which the sales of Nestlé increased 78 percent to 108 billion Swiss francs and its share price increased by more than 300 percent from CHF122 to CHF520. Perhaps the biggest strategic decision Brabeck made during his tenure as CEO was to reposition Nestlé away from a processing-driven food and beverage company toward a broader vision of nutrition, health, and wellness. The logic behind this move was simple enough. Consumers were becoming increasingly aware of the link between food and health and many of Nestlé's products, such as chocolates, ice creams, and frozen foods, contained high levels of sugar. It was a matter of time before consumers moved away from such foods to healthier ones. Nestlé's ambition was to use its knowledge, technologies, and expertise to develop completely new food products. These would be based on ingredi-ents derived from food and would be both nutritional and good for people's health.[1] Unlike medicines that you take after you become ill, the new Nestlé products would stop you from getting ill in the first place. Some would be sold through pharmacies and some through supermarkets.

To make the transition, Nestlé created a separate unit called the Division of Nutrition that reported directly to the CEO. The new unit immediately engaged in a series of acquisitions to establish a platform for growth. For example, it acquired Jenny Craig, a US chain of weight-loss centers, in 2006 and Novartis' Gerber baby foods business in 2007. To support the transi-tion, existing divisions were also required to promote well-being through the development of new products or by improving the nutritional content of their existing products. In the period 2003–2006, Nestlé adjusted recipes to remove 34,000 metric tons of trans fatty acids, 5,000 metric tons of salt, and 204,000 metric tons of sugar from its products.[2] The transition toward health and wellness continued after Brabeck's tenure as CEO ended in 2008.

The new CEO, Paul Bulcke (2008–2017), declared the move as the mainstream of the business and made nutrition the focal point for all the firm's R&D efforts. By the end of his tenure in 2017, Nestlé's product portfolio could boast brands such as Betaquik, a milk-like drink for people with epilepsy; Meritene Regenervis, a flavored drink mix for fatigue and muscle function; Alfamino, for babies and children with food allergies; Peptamen, for digestive health; Renalcal, for acute kidney injury; and Cerefolin, for memory loss. By 2019, the Nutrition and Health Science division was reporting revenues of CHF15 billion.

There is no question that the shift to becoming a nutrition, health, and wellness company represented a radical change for Nestlé and the achievement of CHF15 billion in revenues was no mean feat. However, one cannot fail to notice that this figure represented just 16 percent of Nestlé's 2019 revenues of CHF92.6 billion. Think about this: Auto Trader was able to complete its transition from print to digital within 17 years yet Nestlé achieved less than one-fifth of its migration in the same period of time. Why? Obviously, Nestlé is enormous compared with Auto Trader and we all know how difficult it is to turn a supertanker. Furthermore, the circumstances facing each company were different, so it's not easy to make a direct comparison of their experiences. And Nestlé may legitimately argue that its goal was not to make a clean break from its existing business but to complement it with another business that focused on health and wellness. All these may be valid explanations for the different speed at which these two companies migrated from one strategic position to another. However, these examples also point to another very important factor that determines whether a migration or transition will be successful or not. Specifically, the transition itself and whether it is sustaining or disruptive to the existing core business.

## Is the Transition Disruptive to the Core Business?

What determines the degree of difficulty in making a transition from one strategy to another is not so much how radical the change is—even though that is obviously a factor—but whether the change is disruptive or sustaining to the existing business.[3] A change is sustaining if it improves the existing business; it is disruptive if it undermines or damages it. For example, in response to the digital disruption Walmart introduced several changes in the way the company operated, some of them quite radical.[4] However, most of those changes were sustaining changes in that they were helping improve and grow the existing business. Yes, some of them could be seen as disruptive, especially to those employees who might have lost their jobs as a result of automation, but the amount of disruption involved was limited and manageable. Microsoft, meanwhile, introduced changes that undermined its existing Windows-based business.[5] Not only were resources reallocated away from Windows-based products to build the cloud computing business, but the business model within the existing business was also changed to a subscription model, potentially cannibalizing the Windows business in the process. These are all changes that can only be seen as disruptive in that they are undermining and damaging the existing business. On top of that, the strategic changes also required a fundamental change to the culture of the organization, never an easy matter. In general, the more disruptive the change, the more difficult it is to manage it and the more likely that the transition will take a long time or will even fail.

What makes change disruptive? The word itself gives us a hint—change is disruptive if the new thing we want to do undermines (or disrupts) the existing business or the existing way of doing things. Another way of saying this is that there are conflicts between A (the core business) and B (the new thing), so in attempting to do B, we damage A. The more conflicts there are, the more disruptive the change and the more difficult the transition. Of the many conflicts that might emerge, the following five are by far the most serious.

### The Cannibalization Conflict

When we move from A to B, we are abandoning the revenues and profits of A in search of (hopefully) healthier revenues and profits in B. The problem is that the loss of profits in A is immediate whereas the much-anticipated profits in B may take some time to materialize (if at all). Not only does this create incentives for the managers of the core business A to undermine the transition to B, but it also exposes the firm to stock market pressures. The firm's stock price will most likely take a hit until the revenues and profits in B materialize and compensate for the lost business in A. Consider, for example, the case of Adobe as it contemplated shifting its business model from packaged software to a subscription model: "Adobe's top line revenue would decline as people shifted from a large upfront purchase that could be recognized all in the same quarter, to monthly payments spread out over time. This compression of revenues would take from 24 to 36 months to work through as customers gradually switched from packaged software to online subscriptions. Because Adobe is a publicly traded company, declining revenues and profits were bad for its stock price. And because Adobe was already trading lower against historical averages because of its slower growth, a significant decline in stock price would trigger a takeover bid."[6]

Obviously, there is a fine balancing act that needs to be achieved here, whereby you try to grow B fast enough while at the same time managing the rate of decline in A so that the gains (from B) outweigh the losses (in A). Needless to say, this is an extremely difficult balance to achieve. We only have to look at the nearly fatal attempt by Netflix to migrate from renting DVDs to streaming movies in 2011 to appreciate how real this threat is.[7] The slow pace at which Nestlé migrated to health and wellness may be explained by this factor: You cannot shut down the money-earning part of your business, such as chocolates, frozen food, and ice cream, unless the new business of health and wellness grows fast enough to compensate for the losses. The good news is that there are examples of several companies that managed to pull it off, suggesting that the task may be difficult but not impossible. Adobe is one example of a company that managed to achieve this balance and so are Auto Trader and Netflix. Other examples include Schwab, transitioning to online trading; Nestlé, building up Nespresso at the expense of Nescafé; and the Danish bank Lan & Spar in becoming an online bank.

### The Distribution Conflict

Another potential minefield that might influence the transition from A to B is the distribution conflict. By moving into B, the firm may be undermining the distributors serving A. For example, by moving into online brokerage, Charles Schwab bypassed its own brokers who were used to having the relationship with the end consumers. Similarly, by selling cars online, Auto Trader bypassed the car dealers who traditionally "owned" the customer relationship. By selling Nespresso capsules through the Nespresso Club, Nestlé bypassed its traditional distributors (i.e. supermarkets) on whom it depends to sell its other products. By switching to a subscription model, Adobe was bypassing its two-tier distributor-retail model for a direct-to-consumer one. By offering consumers the ability to subscribe via a phone app to a range of vehicles for a fixed monthly fee via its Passport program, Porsche is bypassing the very dealers on whom it depends to sell its cars. By offering doctors the ability to program the NayaMed pacemakers in an online way through its call center in Lausanne, Switzerland, Medtronic is bypassing its own technical reps, on whom it depends to sell and support its more premium products. The recent conflict between Hollywood studios and movie theater operators illustrates very well what is at stake.[8] In response to the COVID-19 crisis that saw cinemas closed for months in the spring of 2020, studios started releasing movies directly to consumers through digital platforms such as pay-TV and streaming. The success of this forced "experiment" encouraged Universal Studios to announce in April 2020 that it would start releasing films digitally at the same time as it released them to cinemas, in the process breaking one of the industry's established norms of giving the cinemas a three-month advance. This immediately provoked a furious response from the world's two biggest cinema operators, AMC and Cineworld. They issued a global ban on screenings of all films from Universal and accused the studio of breaking the business model that had served the industry well for more than a century.

There are countless examples such as these where the distributors of the existing business may be undermined when a firm attempts to do B. Of course, if the goal is to migrate from A to B, we may be tempted to think that this conflict does not matter. After all, if my goal is to eventually shut down A, what do I care if the distributors in A are upset? This, however, would be a bad assumption to make. The reason this conflict is important is because the existing distributors may not be important *after* you have migrated, but they matter a lot *during* the process of migration. Upsetting distributors during the process of migration will influence the achievement of the fine balance we discussed earlier between the growth of B relative to the decline of A. On the one hand, the distributors will undermine the performance of A, accelerating its decline. On the other hand, bad publicity or problems in A may spill over into B, slowing its growth.

## The Brand Conflict

Another potential issue is the brand conflict whereby the reputation or brand image of A may suffer if the company attempts to do B. One of the key reasons that prevented Harley-Davidson from moving quickly into the market for 70cc motorcycles—a market that propelled Honda to industry leadership—was the fear of damaging the Harley brand. Similarly, by creating Continental Lite to compete against Southwest, Continental was endangering the Continental brand name if things went wrong for the low-cost subsidiary. If the goal is not to migrate from A to B but to operate both A and B simultaneously, a topic covered in Chapter 8, then giving the new business a different name may help. But even this strategy may not eliminate the risk of diluting the brand because customers will not be fooled by just a name change.

## Two Additional Conflicts

Another conflict that might arise in the process of migration is the incentive conflict. The managers of A may feel unfairly treated in that after years of service to the company, they are stuck in the declining part of the business while newly hired people get all the benefits and glory of growing B. Yet another possible conflict is the culture conflict, whereby the managers of A are required to learn to operate in the ways of B if they want to survive within A. For example, moving into a subscription model meant that Microsoft employees needed to change the way they did business, including the way they sold the product, the way they developed new products, and the way they accounted for revenues. This meant they had to shift to a new method of operating while supporting the old ways at the same time. This is extremely difficult and requires that people become ambidextrous. Not only is this likely to lead to mistakes, it could also encourage resistance from people who are used to a certain way of operating.

There are more possible conflicts we could list here, but the point to appreciate is the reason why these conflicts are important for our transition from A to B. As we have already indicated, we need to attract new customers and generate revenues in B at a high enough rate to compensate for the loss of customers in A. Conflicts can influence both items in this equation: On the one hand, they can accelerate the loss of customers and the decline of A; on the other hand, they can slow down the rate at which we attract new customers and so slow down the growth of B. Both of these outcomes will endanger the success of our transition from A to B. We therefore need to find a way to manage these conflicts *during* the migration process.

# How to Manage Conflicts

The most frequent advice given to companies on how to migrate from one strategic position to another, especially when the conflicts between A and B are large, is to create a separate unit as a migration vehicle. This is the "innovator's solution," primarily associated with Clay Christensen's work on disruptive innovation, though other academics have advocated it as well.[9] We discussed this in Chapter 8 in a different context. The issue there was how to compete in both A and B simultaneously and the separate unit was proposed as a way to protect B from the managers of A. The issue we have here is slightly different, specifically how to migrate from A to B by using a separate unit as the vehicle for the transition. Obviously, you will be managing A and B simultaneously during the migration process, so the issues discussed in Chapter 8—such as deciding what activities to separate and what to keep the same, or deciding whether to give the unit a separate name or not—are still relevant here. However, the fact that the goal now is to completely transition from A to B raises a few additional issues, specific to this situation. There are four issues in particular that deserve our attention.

## Allocate Resources Between A and B with Migration in Mind

First, the separate unit is a vehicle for migration and should be treated as such. This means that the firm's resources should be invested over time between A and B with migration in mind. When you start, the majority of the resources are likely to be invested in A, but over time, resources should be slowly reallocated toward B. Every year, a bigger portion of your resources should be invested in B and a smaller portion in A. Remember how Auto Trader described what was happening during its transition from print to digital: "The budget of the print side of the business got reduced every day; the attention it received got reduced every day; its headcount got reduced every day." The plan is to increase the size and importance of B over time while simultaneously decreasing the size and importance of A. If you manage this reallocation of resources and investment well, the time will come when B will become the dominant part of the portfolio. At that time, you could afford to completely shut down A and focus exclusively on B, exactly what Auto Trader did after a 17-year migration process.

This is also the process followed by the Danish bank Lan & Spar but over a much shorter time period. When CEO Peter Schou developed the direct (telephone and then online) bank concept in the early 1990s, he set up a separate direct bank alongside the branch network and kept the two concepts separate for three years before merging them. His rationale was the following: "It was a difficult situation to have two concepts at the same time. We couldn't really afford to merge the two concepts from the very beginning because we would have suffered a huge cannibalization cost. Our interest margin at the branch was 10 percent a year, whereas at the direct bank, it was only 3 percent a year. If we had allowed all of our customers to switch overnight from traditional banking to direct banking, we would have lost a lot of money. We had to manage the transition carefully."

## Prepare B to Take Over

The second issue to address is the fact that the separate unit is a temporary solution and not a permanent feature of the firm's portfolio. Remember, it has been created to help the firm migrate and will cease to exist once the migration has taken place. What this means is that at some point in the future, the separate unit will take over from A and will represent the new strategic position of the firm. This implies that while growing it as a separate unit, we should also prepare it to assume its new role and position in the portfolio. There are several tactics that can be used to achieve this. For example, Charles Schwab had originally set up its online brokerage business called e.Schwab as a separate unit, but prepared it for "taking over" by having it report directly to co-CEO David Pottruck and by staffing it with senior managers from the existing retail organization. In addition, e.Schwab's technology platform was designed to integrate with Schwab's IT systems, and the new unit's product and pricing policies were designed to be compatible with the parent's policies. Similarly, Lan & Spar separated the direct bank from the rest of the organization but made sure that the IT infrastructure that supported the direct bank was compatible with the established bank's IT systems. Furthermore, the bank made sure that the employees developed common values and culture by encouraging common company-wide events. Managers from the main bank were transferred to the direct bank and the decisions on how to merge the two concepts were made in meetings attended by managers from both units.

## Manage the Conflicts Between A and B

The third issue to consider is that the conflicts between A and B do not disappear as a result of creating a separate unit. Yes, separation helps to protect the unit from the conflicts, but it does not eliminate them. They are still there, and they still have to be managed if the transition from A to B is to go smoothly. Again, several tactics can be used to achieve this. Charles Schwab divided its portfolio of products according to complexity. Complex products that required face-to-face interaction with customers were given to brokers to sell while simpler, transaction-based products were moved to the online platform. The company even trained the brokers to do a better job at selling and servicing the higher-margin products. Auto Trader helped overcome the resistance of car dealers by creating selling propositions on its website that worked well for both consumers and dealers. For example, it introduced software that allowed the dealers to service their customers better. NayaMed tried to minimize the resistance of the Medtronic technical reps by focusing its sales efforts on geographic areas and hospitals—small and rural—that the technical reps ignored or simply could not serve. Office Depot changed its incentive systems so that as long as the customer came from the same geographic region as the store, store managers would get rewarded even if a customer purchased products online rather than through the store.

When it comes to brand conflict, many companies adopt the strategy of giving the separate unit a different name, in an effort to reduce the risk of brand dilution. KLM called its low-cost subsidiary Buzz, British Airways called its version Go, and Delta called its offering Song. In the banking industry, Santander called its digital unit Cahoot, RBS called it Bo, and BNP Paribas called it Hello bank! This is not a guarantee of success, however, as the Netflix experience demonstrates. As part of its transition from DVD rentals to movie streaming, Netflix announced in 2011 that the two sides of the business would be separated, and the DVD rental service would be called Quikster. The move backfired with consumers and Netflix quickly killed off the new brand and put the two offerings under the same Netflix brand.

## Separate But Do Not Isolate

The fourth issue to consider is the fact that despite keeping it separate, the unit should not be isolated from the parent.[10] Knowledge and resources should be transferred from A to B to accelerate the process of growing B and so accelerate the transition itself. This will not happen by chance. Integrating mechanisms and processes must be put in place to facilitate knowledge transfer from A to B and to allow better exploitation of synergies between A and B. One such mechanism is to employ a common general manager for both businesses who can provide a holistic approach.[11] Another idea is to appoint an active and credible integrator to facilitate cooperation between the two.[12] Yet another path is to develop incentives that encourage coopera-tion between the two.[13] Transferring people from A to B is also a good way to transfer knowledge and to facilitate cooperation between the two. The separate unit should be allowed to borrow resources and capabilities—such as brand names, customer data, and management expertise—from the core business to gain a competitive advantage over independent start-ups.[14] Sharing value-chain activities with the parent could also help the unit grow more quickly. These could be back-office activities rather than customer-facing ones to allow for efficiencies to be achieved without endangering the unit's ability to differentiate or to cater for its own customers.

The four challenges described here and how the firm manages them will influence to a large extent how long the migration from A to B will take and how successful it will be. It is easy to make mistakes along the way and the experience of Auto Trader highlights this point well. When the separate unit, Autotrader Online, was created in 1996, it was given full autonomy from the parent to grow the digital business. No consideration was given to potential synergies between the print and digital sides of the business, and the leader of the unit, who was an outsider, did not allow anybody from the print side of the business to get close to the unit. The unit adopted a start-up mentality and made it clear that it wanted no input or cooperation from the print business. It did not take long for the magazine side to begin treating the unit as "the enemy" and dysfunctional behaviors surfaced. As one senior executive commented: "We transitioned our revenues online but not our culture and values." At the same time, the targets and KPIs of the unit were encouraging aggressive behaviors, many at the expense of car dealers. For example, the unit would promote products and features—such as reviews of dealers on the website—that consumers liked but dealers hated. Another example of the antagonism with the dealers surfaced during the 2008–2009 recession. This was a period of economic hardship for the car dealers, but despite the difficult economic conditions, Auto Trader proceeded to implement a 30 percent price increase, inflicting more pain on dealers. The relationship got so bad that the dealers organized themselves into a lobby to boycott advertising on the company's website. Even worse, the ten biggest dealers in the UK got together and set up their own website to compete with Auto Trader directly.

Something needed to change, and this happened with the appointment of Trevor Mather as the new CEO in 2013. He immediately changed the focus and attention of the company away from financial results to a new purpose: to lead the digital future of the UK automotive space and to be a trusted leader in the field. Instead of utilizing the five-year plan to drive the print business to zero, he established as the new objective of the plan to serve the changing customer needs and requirements through products that were win-win for the company and for the dealers. Rather than antagonizing dealers, he set out to work with them and to develop products that would help the dealers in pricing their products to the end consumer better. He also embarked on an internal cultural transformation program, trying to create a team that put values such as humility and bravery first. He symbolically changed the name from executive team to leadership team and cut its size from 16 to 8 people. Before even attempting to develop a new strategy, he spent his first few months at the company strengthening the leadership team, improving trust among its members, and working with them to develop the company's new purpose and values. Once a strong and trusting top team was created, they set about developing the new strategy of the company. They also undertook a major cultural transformation program whose goal was to "merge" into one the two cultures that had been created and to help the organization transition online both in revenues and in culture. The top team's obsession with "good growth" and their continuous focus on purpose and values to guide their people's behaviors helped Auto Trader transition successfully into the UK's number one online marketplace for car buyers.

## Other Challenges During the Transition

Managing the conflicts between the existing way of doing business and the new way is not the only challenge facing a firm that attempts to change its strategy. We have focused on this particular challenge in this chapter because many of the others have already been discussed by other management writers and should be well known to leaders. Nevertheless, it may be worthwhile to say a few words about them here.

One of the most challenging tasks facing a leader who is about to embark on a big strategy change is to convince the rest of the organization that moving from A to B is a worthwhile strategic move. Employees need to accept the change not only at a rational level but also at an emotional level. For this to happen, the organization's leaders will have to "sell" the new strategy to their people. We described how to sell something to people to win emotional commitment in Chapter 6 (Figure 6.1). That same framework can be used here to think how to sell the new strategy. Whether we succeed in selling the new strategy will depend not only on how we try to do it but on four additional factors. We described these factors in Chapter 3 (Figure 3.4); consideration must be given to all of them to increase the probability of success. In addition to employees, other external stakeholders such as shareholders will have to be convinced to support the change of strategy. Having a clear plan that specifies how the new strategy will play out over time and what key milestones (such as sales or profits) will be achieved along the way is one tactic to convince skeptical shareholders. Another even more persuasive tactic is data from experimentation. There is nothing more persuasive for both employees and shareholders than data which supports the key elements of the new strategy, so clever experiments should be designed to provide the necessary supporting data. We described in Chapter 9 how to carry out clever and low-cost experiments.

Another challenge to overcome is how to change the organizational environment of the company to support the new strategy. As we described in Chapter 4, the organizational environment is made up of four elements— the organization's culture and values, its measurement and incentives, its structures and processes, and its people. These four elements combine to determine how people behave in the organization and this in turn determines whether our strategy will be supported or undermined by the day-to-day behaviors of our employees. Every strategy needs its own supporting organizational environment. This means that if we are to change from strategy A to strategy B, we simultaneously need to change the organizational environment that was supporting A to one that will support B. Thus, we will need to recruit new people who possess the skills and mindsets appropriate for our new strategy or train our existing people to develop the new skills and mindsets. We will also have to change our measurement and incentive systems as well as our structures and processes to support the new strategy. Finally, we will have to change the culture and values of the organization to the ones that fit the new strategy. This is a tall order and that may explain why strategic change takes such a long time or why it is so often associated with failure.

Finally, there is the issue of assessing whether the new strategy is performing according to expectations and if not, whether it needs to be changed or abandoned altogether. Obviously, the financial results of the new strategy relative to what was projected on the plan at the beginning of the transition can be a good indicator of whether we are on track as planned. But it is usually better to supplement the indicators of financial health (such as revenues and profits relative to the plan) with a few indicators of the company's strategic health, such as customer satisfaction, employee morale, new products in the pipeline, and quality of management. The company needs to develop indicators of strategic health appropriate for its context and use its information systems to collect the necessary data to measure these indicators on a regular basis. As long as the indicators of strategic health are good, the company can persist in its migration, even if the financial results are not going according to plan. Ultimately, this decision will require the organization's leaders to use their judgment and this is the topic we turn to next.

# References

**1** Matthew Campbell and Corinne Gretler: "Nestlé wants to sell you both sugary snacks and diabetes pills," *Bloomberg.com*, May 5, 2016.

**2** David E. Bell and Mary Shelman: "Nestlé," Harvard Business School case study 9-509-001, revised October 15, 2012.

**3** The terms sustaining and disruptive were coined by Clayton Christensen in his work on disruptive innovation. See Clayton Christensen: *The Innovator's Dilemma*, Boston, MA: Harvard Business School Press, 1997.

**4** Elliot Maras: "An insider's view of Wal Mart's digital transformation," *Retail Customer Experience*, February 21, 2019; Pamela Danziger: "Wal Mart doubles down on its transformation into a technology company," *Forbes*, October 22, 2018.

**5** Richard Waters: "FT Person of the Year: Satya Nadella," *Financial Times*, December 18, 2019.

**6** Charlene Li: *The Disruption Mindset*, Washington, DC: IdeaPress Publishing, 2019, p. 47.

**7** Ibid, p. 41.

**8** Mark Sweney: "Studios bypass cinemas with lucrative lockdown premieres," *The Guardian*, UK edition, May 2, 2020.

**9** Clayton Christensen: *The Innovator's Dilemma: When new technologies cause great firms to fail*, Boston, MA: Harvard Business School Press, 1997; Clark Gilbert and Joseph Bower: "Disruptive change: When trying harder is part of the problem," *Harvard Business Review*, May 2002, pp. 3–8; Clark Gilbert, Matthew Eyring, and Richard Foster: "Two routes to resilience," *Harvard Business Review*, December 2012.

**10** B. Harreld: "Which businesses to grow? Which not?" *Across the Board*, November–December 2004, pp. 9–10.

**11** Charles O'Reilly III and Michael Tushman: "The ambidextrous organization," *Harvard Business Review*, 2004, Vol. 82, No. 4, pp. 74–81.

**12** Clark Gilbert and Joseph Bower: "Disruptive change: When trying harder is part of the problem," *Harvard Business Review*, May 2002, pp. 3–8.

**13** Sumantra Ghoshal and Lynda Gratton: "Integrating the enterprise," *Sloan Management Review*, 2003, Vol. 44, No. 1, pp. 31–38.

**14** VG Govindarajan and Chris Trimble: *Ten Rules for Strategic Innovators: From idea to execution*, Boston, MA: HBS Press, 2005.

# 11

# Putting It All Together

In the first chapter, I outlined the kinds of questions that this book will answer for the reader. It may be worthwhile to finish the book by listing these questions again and giving a concise answer for each.

- The first question posed in Chapter 2 was: "How should you frame disruption to your people, as a threat or as an opportunity?" The answer we gave was "as both a threat and an opportunity." We explained why this is so important and then raised the supplementary question: "How can you convince people that something is an opportunity when all they see around them are the threats associated with disruption?" Our answer was that you need to go beyond telling them that this is the case to *selling them* the idea that disruption is indeed an opportunity. This requires the use of not only words but also concrete actions that demonstrate that you are serious when you say that disruption is an opportunity. We used the example of KBC Bank to illustrate this point.

- In Chapter 3 we posed the question: "How do you create a *permanent* sense of urgency or a *constant* unease with the status quo, no matter how successful the status quo may be?" Our answer was that scaring people through a burning platform will not do the trick. You will need to make the need for change personal and emotional. To do this, you will have to give your people something positive to aim for and then sell it to them to win emotional commitment. We outlined a few tactics to win emotional commitment and described the factors that will affect your selling effectiveness.

- Chapter 4 explored the question: "How do you make the organization agile enough to identify and respond to whatever disruption hits you?" Our answer was that agility is not something we can ask or demand of people. It is, instead, a by-product of something else—specifically, the day-to-day behaviors associated with agility that each and every employee engages in. We described what these behaviors are, but then raised the follow-up question: "How can we make sure that our employees behave like this on a daily basis?" The answer is that it is the organizational environment that determines how people behave, so we need to put in place an organizational environment that supports and promotes these behaviors.

- In Chapter 5 we asked the question: "How can we create such a supportive organizational environment? Our answer was that most companies try to do this in a centralized way, from the top down. We argued for a different approach: Individual managers and team leaders scattered all over the organization can achieve major changes in their local organizational environments through a few small and targeted actions. Done within prescribed parameters as set by top management, these decentralized actions could start a thousand little fires that can grow into an inferno that transforms the organizational environment of the whole company. We described a few of these "small actions" that can lead to big changes.

- Chapter 6 argued that the proposed decentralized approach to changing the organizational environment cannot succeed unless clear parameters are put in place to guide individual managers and team leaders in deciding what they can do and what they should not do without top management approval. We therefore asked the question: "What are these parameters within which we allow our people to act with autonomy?" Our answer was that there are two such parameters: the organization's clearly communicated strategy, and the organization's values and purpose. We further argued that even though there is nothing surprising in this answer, the evidence is that organizations consistently and predictably mess up the implementation of both. We explained why and what to do about it.

- In Chapter 7 we posed the question: "What specific strategy should the organization adopt in response to disruption?" Our answer was that this depends on the specific disruption to which we are responding. However, whatever the disruption, an effective strategy of response must avoid imitating what others have done in response to the disruption and should instead help the firm differentiate itself as much as possible. Simply trying to be better than the disruptors themselves or industry rivals responding to the same disruption is not enough. In this sense, the firm is not looking for a strategy of response—it is looking for a strategy that will allow it to reposition and differentiate itself by taking advantage of the disruption.

- Chapter 8 explored the question: "How can an organization develop such a truly innovative strategy of response?" We argued that how you approach the task is as important as what strategy is adopted. We specifically proposed that companies need to start their thinking like an entrepreneur in order to avoid the myopia of their core business. In developing a response strategy, we proposed a structured approach to develop ideas, one that requires the firm to identify ways to do four things: exploit disruptors' weaknesses; borrow good ideas from disruptors without imitating them; eliminate things made unnecessary by disruption; and innovate in how and where to compete. We further argued that creativity is enhanced if the principle of variety is institutionalized in the strategy process of the organization and we described how to do this.

- In Chapter 9 we posed the question: "How do you know if your strategy of response is a good one and how do you convince the rest of the organization to follow you in implementing it?" The answer we gave is that experimentation can be an effective way to both test a new strategy and collect data that will help convince others to accept it. However, we also pointed out that not all experiments are good experiments. How do you make sure you design and carry out a "good" experiment, especially when it comes to dealing with a new strategy? We described what clever experimentation looks like and discussed how to create a culture of experimentation in the organization.

- Finally, Chapter 10 explored the question: "How do you make the transition from your existing strategy A to your new strategy of response B?" We argued that any change from A to B is difficult, but some changes are more difficult than others. What determines the degree of difficulty is not so much how radical the change is—even though that is obviously a factor—but whether the change is disruptive or sustaining to the existing business. We explained what makes change disruptive and offered some ideas for how to overcome the problems and conflicts created when the move to B is disruptive to A.

As I pointed out early in the book, I hope that senior executives do not find these ideas surprising, and there should be nothing here that they do not immediately recognize. However, knowing what to do is not the same thing as doing it or doing it correctly. How you implement these ideas will be the difference between success and failure. As a result, my emphasis has been to offer practical, research-based insights on how to put into action some of the things you probably already know. Rather than develop a new recipe for success, the book has focused on the "how to." It may be helpful, therefore, to finish with an example of an organization that utilized some of these ideas to prepare itself for a world of continuous disruption. This organization is Belgium's KBC Bank. In reading through this example, ask yourselves: "How did this organization *implement* (a few of) the ideas proposed in this book to prepare for a world of continuous disruption?"

## The Experience of KBC Bank

In 2016, Belgium's KBC Bank announced a new, comprehensive groupwide digital transformation initiative. Labelled the "Digital First" transformation, the group's CEO Johan Thijs described it as the bank's attempt to not only look to the future and prepare for it but also shape that future by developing new and revolutionary ways for customers to do their banking. The vision was to use digital technologies as well as big data and analytics to offer the customer products and solutions that they had not even thought about, and to deliver them to consumers in an easy, consumer-friendly, digital way. In Thijs' own words: "I want to know what you as a customer are thinking and how you are spending your time and money. Based on that, I want to be able to develop solutions to your everyday problems and offer these solutions to you before you even know you needed them. That's what Google is doing, and we need to be as good as them in doing this. Because our customers don't dream about the bank, we need to be in their heads and be their default option before they buy something. But we must also go beyond this. I always say to my staff, be aware, you sell trust. That's the only thing you cannot digitalize. That's our opportunity to go beyond what even Google can offer the customer."

The transformation initiative was noteworthy not only for its ambition but also for its timing. It was announced when the bank was enjoying a period of excellent performance, following a near-fatal experience in the 2008 financial crisis. This is how a financial magazine described the decision: "For a banking giant such as KBC—one that consistently posts profits that are among the *very* strongest in the European market, and one that is always highly liquid and well-capitalised—it may not have been the most obvious or pressing decision in the world to embark on such a journey, especially given the clear leadership position it had attained under its prevailing business model. Indeed, the proverb 'If it ain't broke, don't fix it' immedi-ately springs to mind; moreover, attempting to convince the group's 42,000-strong employee base that their winning business model must be significantly enhanced could not have been the easiest of tasks."[1]

Three years later, the transformation was rated a roaring success. For example, an external assessment in 2018 by D-Rating, an independent agency that rates digital performance, ranked KBC as the best-performing tradi-tional bank in Belgium, based on a series of indicators that measured the digitization of banks' offerings, the efficiency of contact channels, and the performance of customer journeys. Johan Thijs had no doubt what the foun-dation for this success was. He credited his people for proactively anticipating customers' changing behaviors and then taking personal responsibility for developing solutions quickly and without too much bureaucracy. He said: "The translation of responsiveness is you proactively anticipate... the fulfil-ment of customer needs. So, you have to anticipate customers' changing behavior...[and then] you are allowed to anticipate and help us understand what we have to do. So, you are empowered to provide the solution, which is happening big time in our group."[2] These were impressive behaviors from KBC employees, but how did Thijs and his management team get them to behave in such admirable ways? To answer this question, we have to go back to 2012, the year Thijs was appointed group CEO. The first strategic action he took in his new role was to embark on a major transformation of the bank's culture. The groupwide culture change program was called PEARL, which stood for Performance, Empowerment, Accountability, Responsiveness, and Local embeddedness.

Thijs had been a KBC insider for most of his career. He came from the insurance side of the business and rose to become the managing director of the Belgium subsidiary in 2009 before becoming group CEO in 2012. He had seen the evolution and growth of the bank over the years and had become convinced that KBC had lost the entrepreneurial spirit on which it had built its original success. Processes had become overly complex, and projects were often delayed through indecision or inertia. Employees behaved in risk-averse ways and were quick to avoid personal ownership of issues, shifting the blame for mistakes to outside forces. Decision making throughout the bank was dysfunctional in that decisions were often made in corridors rather than in teams. This was equally true in the group executive committee (ExCo), which was characterized by extreme conservatism, as well as back-door decision making. A senior executive at the time described the situation as unbelievably frustrating: "There were silos run by powerful managing directors, corporate governance was not very strong, and there was a lack of accountability at the level of the executive committee. The mentality was 'I won't challenge you, if you don't challenge me.' Executive committee meetings were very short, and things happened without people knowing about it." In addition, misaligned incentives were encouraging behaviors that undermined the strategy and performance of the bank. For example, Thijs' early investigations revealed an alarming lack of accountability on the part of his managers, made possible by the total lack of awareness of the profitability of each product sold by the bank. Pursuing this further, he discovered: "Our sales and distribution people were being measured and incentivized according to sales rather than profits. As a result, their goal was market share, not profitability. If they sold something that did not make any money for the bank, it wasn't their problem. In addition, since they were not responsible for the products they were selling, if things went wrong, they had no control over the situation." On top of everything, there was a strong disconnect and a lack of engagement between employees and management. It was obvious that employees had lost all trust in management, were demotivated and unhappy, and blamed senior management for all the problems the group was facing.

Thijs was determined to change this and made it his first priority as the new CEO: to develop a culture that would encourage entrepreneurial behaviors and a new mindset across the entire group. He came up with the concept of PEARL, which emphasized performance and responsiveness as outcomes that would emerge from empowerment, accountability, and local embeddedness. Although PEARL originated from the ExCo, Thijs wanted employees to implement it from within, without any help from consultants. His ambition was that employees would immerse themselves in their local environment, understand the needs of their local customers, and respond to them directly, without referring to the corporate center. They could do all this as long as they operated within the parameters of the PEARL framework, which meant that these parameters had to be clearly communicated to the whole organization. Effectively, the ExCo decided on the strategic priorities for the group and then all tactical decisions were taken by a business development committee (per business/segment), headed by a member of the executive committee. Operational decisions would be taken even further down the organization. Decentralization was the major pillar of Thijs' CEO candidature presentation and he credited it as part of the reason he was chosen for the role, while all the other candidates offered centralized solutions. Thijs strongly believed that since local businesses understood local customer needs better, they should have the autonomy to make decisions. This would lead to quicker and better service to customers.

Decentralization and empowerment were at the heart of the new culture, but so was an emphasis on making decisions quickly. For example, employees were encouraged to avoid meetings and instead use information available for discussion and comment on the intranet. At a certain date, unless there was a fundamental objection, it was taken that there was general agreement on issues posted, which were then actioned. Documents compiled for discussion in ExCo meetings were also under scrutiny to be PEARL compliant. This resulted in shorter, focused documents that presented the facts and analysis in a clear and concise way, rather than pages of narrative that would take hours to read. In addition, the new culture promoted the creation of agile teams, composed of people who could take decisions confidently and put in motion initiatives that were necessary to ensure that customers' needs were fulfilled. People were held accountable for their decisions. Thijs did not mind if people made mistakes, as long as they took ownership of their decisions and learned from mistakes.

At the same time as launching PEARL, Thijs announced a new performance management system called the Performance Diamond. The four segments of the diamond were capital, liquidity, profitability, and people. Targets were set for these four dimensions for each country and for each business entity in each country. Local management could act in any way they wanted to meet the targets set for each of the four dimensions, but their actions had to be within the specified boundaries decided by ExCo. This was a central element of empowerment. If management were not performing within the parameters, then they were asked to explain what was happening. Thijs explained: "Before I took over, everything was centrally driven. For example, the group would say, 'You have to use this ICT system.' In some of the smaller countries they didn't need something as complex but they had no choice. At the end of each year they would receive an invoice from the group for the cost of the services that were provided, such as ICT. Often this decision that was imposed on them would result in their cost ratio being completely wiped out. Things like this completely removed any feeling of responsibility from local managers. That's why we changed it all and devolved power. With devolved power came a sense of personal accountability. Local responsiveness was key and now business managers began to feel responsible for what they are doing. The center doesn't have to interfere anymore."

PEARL and the Performance Diamond were quickly rolled out across the businesses and soon started developing islands of energy and best practice across the organization. To help managers who were not used to operating in this autonomous way, coaching, tools, and training were offered. The new culture took hold quickly and the financial results soon followed. KBC was able to repay five years ahead of schedule all bailouts it had received from the Belgian and Flemish governments during the 2008 financial crisis, and its share price tripled within three years of Thijs taking over. A report in the *Financial Times* in 2015 commented on this dramatic turnaround: "The turnaround is most pronounced at KBC as it shakes off its crisis funk... steady profit generation has worked wonders for capital generation... Keep up that pace and KBC's targets of repaying the state by year-end and paying dividends from 2016 begin to look conservative. Already on 1.8 times tangible book value for a return on equity of 17%, KBC is fast gaining the highly rated attributes of Scandinavia's banks. Try naming other European banks in the same position."[3]

The success of the cultural transformation did not surprise Thijs. This was because he had done something similar before. In 2009, when he took over as managing director of the Belgium subsidiary, he set in motion a cultural transformation there, based on the same principles of empowerment and accountability. He described his decision to change the culture at the Belgian business unit as follows: "On a Sunday afternoon, I went home and I started to write the 'umbrella' that would guide my people. I called it SLIM. This word means 'slim' in English, but it means 'smart' in Dutch. SLIM meant you will do business according to common sense not according to rules. If the rules are stupid, don't follow the rules! It's your responsibility to deliver, but if it goes wrong you can blame it on the SLIM culture—it's on my account." In small ways, SLIM started to change the thinking and mindsets of employees. It encouraged them to take the initiative and to change things without fear of failure. Just because something was done in a certain way for years did not mean that it was untouchable. Employees were encouraged to challenge everything and develop new and more customer-friendly ways to do things that would have a significant impact on KBC and its customers. The success of this initiative in the Belgian subsidiary reinforced Thijs' belief in its underpinning principles and acted as the blueprint for the introduction of PEARL in the whole group, three years later. Seven years on, Thijs was crediting the success of his digital transformation during 2016–2020 to the PEARL culture. In June 2020, a new four-year strategy was announced and Thijs was confident that in 2025, he would, once again, be giving credit for yet another successful transformation to this same culture. As he put it, once you get the DNA of the organization right, you can be confident that everything that follows will be fundamentally fine. At that point, all you have to do as a leader is to sit back and watch your people thrive.

What has guided Thijs' actions over the years is a "customer-first" mentality. He said: "We have to always remember that the reason we exist is for our customers. We are here to give them advice on everything that matters to them and to be a part of their life. As long as we live by this principle, then it is pretty obvious what the bank has to do: just adapt to the changes in customer needs and expectations." As is evident by the day-to-day behaviors of employees, this principle resides not only in Thijs' head but also in the culture of the organization. For example, in deciding what new products to offer or how to interact with customers, employees would start their team meetings by reflecting on how they, as consumers, were using technology in their home lives. They would ask questions such as: How do we do our shopping every day? How do we search for information? How do we communicate with friends? How do we feel if our order from Amazon takes more than 24 hours to arrive? How often do we use Siri or Alexa? How differently from us do our children use technology? And so on. Based on these insights, they then decide what the bank needs to do by asking questions such as "What does all this mean for our bank? What should we change here to fit into the life of these consumers?" This constant focus on customers and a passion to deliver the best customer experience in the world is what guides the bank's actions and is credited as the primary reason for its continuous success over the years.

## What Can We Learn From KBC?

The KBC example is a nice way to summarize the key elements that make up the answer to the question posed by this book: how does an organization prepare for a journey of continuous disruption? As discussed in Chapter 4, a key step is to make the organization agile enough to identify and respond to whatever disruption hits us. How can we do this? Certainly not by asking people to be agile! Instead, we should encourage everybody in the organization to adopt the day-to-day behaviors that will lead to agility. Agility is not something we can ask of people. It is, instead, a by-product of something else—specifically, the day-to-day behaviors that will make us agile. Consider how KBC achieved this. By encouraging employees to stay close to the customers (i.e. local embeddedness), to anticipate their changing behaviors (i.e. responsiveness), to take ownership in developing solutions (i.e. accountability), and to do so on their own initiative (i.e. empowerment), Thijs has put in place the ingredients of an agile organization. But how did he "encourage" his people to adopt these behaviors? As we have pointed out, people do not behave in these wonderful ways simply because we tell them to, even when they know it is the right thing to do. To get these behaviors, we must first create the organizational environment that will support and promote them. By this we mean the culture as well as the incentives, structures, processes, and people that support the behaviors of agility. This was exactly what Thijs focused on through the PEARL cultural transformation of the bank. By putting this organizational environment in place in 2012, he was able to undertake one major transformation at the bank in 2012–2016, another one in 2016–2020, and is confident that this same environment will nurture the transformation of 2020–2025. As he said, once you get the DNA of the organization right, you can be confident that everything that follows will be fundamentally fine.

As we also argued in Chapter 5, creating the organizational environment that supports and promotes the behaviors of agility does not necessarily have to be done in a centralized way and does not have to be undertaken by top management alone. Individual managers scattered all over the organization can achieve major changes in their local organizational environments through a few small and targeted actions. Done properly, these decentralized actions could start a thousand little fires that can grow into an inferno that transforms the organizational environment of the whole company. This was what Thijs did at KBC, but as we argued in Chapter 6, the decentralized approach to changing the organizational environment cannot succeed unless clear parameters are put in place to guide individual managers and team leaders as to what they can do and what they should not do without top management approval. There are two types of parameters that can be used: the organization's clearly communicated strategy, and the organization's values and purpose. As argued so passionately by Johan Thijs, the purpose that has guided autonomy and initiative-taking at KBC over the years has been "customers first." This has been ingrained in the DNA of the organization and acts as the North Star for KBC, no matter what transformation it is undertaking.

The purpose of KBC served a second role—it created a perennial discomfort with the status quo and gave employees a positive reason to strive for change. Since customer needs and expectations change all the time, the implication was that KBC also had to change all the time to keep ahead of customers and to honor its purpose. In Chapters 2–3, we argued that to prepare the organization for continuous change, we must first frame disruption as both a threat and an opportunity, but then spend most of our time and energy trying to convince people that it is, indeed, an opportunity. We also argued that we must create the right kind of urgency in the organization by giving people a positive goal to aim for and then making the need for change personal and emotional. The purpose of KBC represents a positive goal to aim for and presents the need for change as an opportunity to pursue. Of course, Thijs still needed to "sell" this goal to his people to win their emotional commitment. We don't know whether he did this or how, but judging by the results, we can be confident that people bought into it.

## The Ingredients for Successful Transformation

What we have outlined so far are important reasons for the success of KBC's numerous transformations over the years. Of course, this is not an exhaustive list—for example, we did not examine the specific *strategies* that KBC adopted over the years, and obviously they are also important ingredients of success. There are many factors that influence the outcome of any transformation attempt and I believe that most of these factors can be placed in three broad categories. As shown in Figure 11.1, these are the WHY, WHAT and HOW of transformation. The WHY is the reason we give to our people for undertaking yet another transformation. This reason needs to be a positive one and needs to be "sold" to people so that they buy into it. The WHAT is the strategy that we will adopt. This is specific to the disruption we are responding to, but in general, it has to be innovative and must allow us to not just defend against the disruption but also exploit it. In addition, this strategy must be clearly communicated to our people so as to win their buy-in. The HOW refers to the organizational support required to execute the strategy of response. This involves the development of an organizational environment that promotes the behaviors of agility and supports the chosen strategy.

FIGURE 11.1    The ingredients for successful transformation

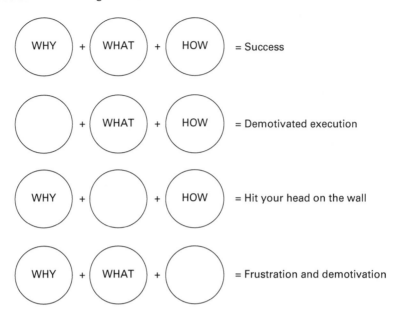

If all three elements are put in place, the probability of success is high. If we put two of the three in place but the WHY is missing, we are likely to get demotivated execution of our strategy. If the WHAT is missing while the other two are in place, we will get lots of motivated and excited people hitting their heads on the wall. If the HOW is missing while the other two are in place, we will have a frustrated and demotivated organization. If two—any two—of the three are missing, failure is almost guaranteed. Needless to say, for the correct development and implementation of all three, a prerequisite is strong leadership. But that is a topic for another book.

## References

1   John Manning: "For KBC, Europe's leading bank-insurer, digital first means customer first," *International Banker*, April 1, 2019.
2   Ibid.
3   Lex: "High hopes for banking in the low countries", *Financial Times*, May 18, 2015.

# INDEX

Page numbers in *italic* indicate figures or tables.